P-51 MUST

SEVENTY-FIVE YEARS of AMERICA'S MOST F

CORY GRAFF

ANG

OUS WARBIRD

ZENITH
PRESS

CORY GRAFF has nearly twenty years of experience working in aviation museums, creating exhibits, conducting historical research, and educating visitors. He is currently the military aviation curator at the world-famous Flying Heritage Collection and has previously worked at the Museum of Flight and collaborated with the Whatcom Museum of History and Art, the Frye Art Museum, the Washington State History Museum, the Puget Sound Navy Museum, and the Museum of Glass. Graff is the author of nine books on various aviation and military history subjects, most recently *Flying Warbirds*, published by Zenith Press in 2014. He has also co-created four additional books with museums and private publishers and has written for *Air & Space/Smithsonian*, *Air Classics*, *Alof* magazine, and *Warbirds International*. www.corygraff.com

First published in 2015 by Zenith Press, an imprint of Quarto Publishing Group USA Inc., 400 First Avenue North, Suite 400, Minneapolis, MN 55401 USA

Zenith Press titles are also available at discounts in bulk quantity for industrial or sales-promotional use. For details write to Special Sales Manager at Quarto Publishing Group USA Inc., 400 First Avenue North, Suite 400, Minneapolis, MN 55401 USA.

To find out more about our books, visit us online at www.zenithpress.com.

Library of Congress Cataloging-in-Publication Data

Graff, Cory, 1971-
  P-51 Mustang : seventy-five years of America's most famous warbird / Cory Graff.
    pages cm
  Includes index.
  ISBN 978-0-7603-4859-8 (hbk.)
  1. Mustang (Fighter plane)--History. I. Title.
  UG1242.F5G663 2015
  623.74'64--dc23
                    2015018209

Acquring Editor: Erik Gilg
Project Manager: Madeleine Vasaly
Art Director: James Kegley
Cover Designer: John Barnett/4Eyes Design
Layout Designer: Rebecca Pagel

On the front cover:
Colonel William Banks, commander of the 348th Fighter Group, flies Sunshine VII in the last weeks of World War II. The rainbow nose on the P-51K carried the color of each of the four squadrons within the group, and the large black stripes on the airplane helped in quick recognition from nearly any angle.
The Norm Taylor Collection/The Museum of Flight

On the back cover:
Patches for the Fifteenth, Seventh, and Eighth Air Force.

On the endpapers:
A flight of 31st Fighter Group Mustangs, loaded with fuel, go out looking for trouble. The month before, in July 1944, the group had destroyed eighty-two German airplanes. In August, they flew escort for three bombing missions to the Ploesti oil fields in Romania. *National Archives*

Frontispiece:
Loaded down for a flight to Tokyo, a pair of 506th Fighter Group Mustangs sticks close to their navigational B-29. This image was taken out the gunnery bubble on the side of the bomber. While the Mustangs attacked targets, the B-29 crew would loiter offshore, ready to pick up the P-51s and take them back home to Iwo Jima. *National Archives*

On the title pages:
The long line of Mustangs rolls on into infinity. On an average day, NAA built twenty of the big fighters. In 1945, there were a couple of months during which NAA produced more than thirty on each workday. To make this photo even more impressive, look closely—there is another line of Mustangs behind the first! *Santa Maria Museum of Flight*

Printed in China

10 9 8 7 6 5 4 3 2 1

CONTENTS

FOREWORD

The P-51 Mustang is one of the most iconic aircraft in aviation history and arguably the most important plane that took to the skies in World War II. From its inception to its rollout in less than 120 days, it was bound to become a legend.

My interest in airplanes came at the age of six when my father took me to see *The Hunters*, a Korean War film featuring the North American F-86 Sabre Jet. The movie inspired me at this very young age to build models and read aircraft histories. Needless to say, there is no better-looking fighter than the P-51, so my interest in knowing more about this beautiful airplane was inevitable.

In second grade I became friends with Jim Maloney, whose father, Ed Maloney, had just opened the Air Museum—now called the Planes of Fame Air Museum—near my home in Claremont, California. The museum had an F-86 and a P-51 on display in a small, humble building that allowed Jim and me to get close to the real airplanes I had read about. At only eight years old, there wasn't much we could do except pick up around the museum, but the reward for doing so was being allowed, occasionally, to sit in some of the aircraft.

The P-51 there was given the name *Spam Can* by Ed Maloney's friend and World War II P-47 Thunderbolt ace Walker "Bud" Mahurin, who also flew F-86s in Korea. (The name was what jet pilots affectionately called prop fighters in the 1950s.) *Spam Can*, which was flown occasionally, was a beautiful plane.

When I graduated from high school with plans of becoming an airline pilot, flying the Mustang was at the top of my wish list. I earned my private ticket at eighteen and flew every airplane I could get my hands on. Jim and I were allowed to pilot the museum's T-6, and we flew it as much as we could in order to gain experience enough to reach our ultimate goal of flying the Mustang. At the same time, we both worked at any airplane-related job we could find to keep the T-6 gas money flowing. It seemed like an eternity, but after two years and three hundred hours of flying time, Jim and I finally got to fly *Spam Can.*

As twenty-year-olds who flew the Mustang, we gained a lot of notoriety as "the Chino Kids," and that afforded us many opportunities. We met and worked with people from all over the country because of it. Today, fifty-six years after seeing *The Hunters*, I have flown more than two thousand pilot-in-command hours in more than fifty different P-51s, including the highly modified P-51 *Red Baron*, in which I won four Unlimited Air Races and set the World Speed Record for piston-powered propeller-driven aircraft at 499.047 miles per hour. The record was formerly held by Darryl Greenameyer, and before him Howard Hughes and Jimmy Doolittle, to name a few.

Since 1980, my company has rebuilt forty warbirds, including twelve P-51 Mustangs for collectors in the United States and England. But I haven't flown only Mustangs. To coin a phrase, the P-51 has truly been the skeleton key to aviation for me, opening doors to friendships with so many outstanding individuals, pilots like Jim and John Maloney, LeRoy Penhall, Frank Sanders, John Sandberg, Jim Gavin, and Bill and John Muszala; veterans like Bud Mahurin, Bob Hoover, Paul Poberezny, Bob Love, and Bud Anderson; and collectors like Stephen Grey, Tom and Dan Friedkin, Bob Pond, and Rod Lewis.

The most amazing Mustang story in my life is the fact that my son Steve "Stevo" Hinton has taken the reins and continues to raise the bar in the P-51 history books again. At the young age of twenty-two, he won the Reno Air Races flying a modified P-51 named *Strega*. To date, he has raced two different racing P-51s to six consecutive unlimited victories.

Some fifty years after I first saw the Mustang, I am still excited and amazed about the history of how this plane came to be, its design and development, and its deployment and service history. Meeting the men and women who flew them and built them has been a highlight of my life. The contribution the P-51 has made to world history and its continued life into our modern world is unparalleled. Cory's seventy-fifth anniversary book is the ultimate testament to this iconic plane; I hope you enjoyed reading it as much as me.

Happy flying.

—Steve Hinton, April 2015

Steve Hinton is the president of the Planes of Fame Museum and the owner of Fighter Rebuilders in Chino, California. He is a test pilot, air-show performer, World Speed Record holder, and Reno Air Race Champion who also operates vintage warbirds for the motion-picture industry. Hinton has logged more than 11,500 hours in the air, including 9,000 hours in more than 150 types of vintage aircraft.

Above: A pair of 506th Fighter Group Mustangs cruise near Iwo Jima. *The Boll Weevil* and 599 (called *Anything Goes*) served in the same group, but different squadrons, hence the different tails. The airplane in the foreground was with the 457th Fighter Squadron (green tail) and 599 was assigned to the 458th Fighter Squadron (blue stripes). *National Archives*

Left: Before being wrapped for overseas shipment, workers "mask" a Mustang, carefully covering each seam. The P-51D was bound for the Pacific when it was photographed in November 1944. *National Archives*

INTRODUCTION

AMERICA'S MOST FAMOUS FIGHTER

THE STORY OF THE P-51 MUSTANG has always been a popular one. There are few, if any, airplanes of the World War II era that carry more myth and mystique. Along with the aircraft carrier and the jeep, the Mustang is often credited with truly changing the outcome of the largest conflict in human history.

The tale of the P-51 is appealing because there are many great stories within it; the workers at North American Aviation (NAA) took to the task of duplicating a painfully ordinary airplane and turned it into so much more. They worked for just a few short months in 1941 and came up with one of the all-time greatest airplanes. However, nothing is created in a vacuum, and this airplane was not perfected without a little help from a top-end European car company turned powerplant manufacturer extraordinaire.

In battle, P-51s slogged through sandstorms and monsoons, overflying oceans, mountains, jungles, and endless miles of the

Over the California coast, NAA shows off its 20mm-armed Mustang for an aerial photographer. The long-barreled Hispano cannons were belt fed and carried 125 rounds per gun—only about ten seconds of firing before all the ammunition was gone. *Stan Piet Collection*

Above: Movie pilot and actor Tom Friedkin owns *Double Trouble Two*, a beautifully restored P-51D (44-73856). The airplane's N-Number, required by the Federal Aviation Administration, can be seen in very small lettering hidden under the Mustang's horizontal stabilizer. *Gavin Conroy*

Inset: The US Army Air Forces (USAAF) shoulder-sleeve insignia was designed by a member of Gen. Henry "Hap" Arnold's staff in 1942. It features a winged US national insignia over an "ultramarine disk"— representative of "the medium in which the Air Forces operated." *Author's Collection*

war-torn world below. With the help of enterprising mechanics and ground crews and their beautifully simple, jettisonable fuel tanks, it seemed that Mustangs could appear anywhere at any time. And over Berlin or Tokyo, thousands of miles from home, Mustang pilots could go toe-to-toe with anything they encountered in the skies and usually return victorious.

Years later and well past its prime, the P-51 was relegated to the inglorious job of hauling bombs in East Asia. The plane was used up by a nation that had moved on to faster and better combat machines. And if you want to see a warbird enthusiast reduced to tears, talk about the 1960s, when one could buy a "complex and expensive-to-operate" surplus P-51 Mustang for just a few hundred dollars. In those days, many people thought it was economical and smart to chop up this old airplane for scrap aluminum.

The fighter's status as a beautiful icon and champion of World War II coupled with the dark days of Korean War destruction and the purge of surplus airplanes that soon followed are what make a Mustang such a valuable commodity today. Less than 2 percent of the 15,586 examples of the P-51 and its A-36 variant survive.

Today, seventy-five years after the Mustang's first flight, it wouldn't be quite true to say that a P-51 is worth its weight in gold. The ridiculous notion that an old machine, built to last for a few weeks in combat, could be worth as much as the best-known precious metal is hyperbole of the highest order. However, a Mustang commonly sells for around $2 million today—if you sit down and really crunch the numbers, amazingly, an NAA P-51 Mustang is quite literally worth its weight in silver.

This airplane, widely considered one of the best fighters ever built, is the foundation of any aviation museum collection. At the time of this writing, more than 150 P-51s are registered with the Federal Aviation Administration in the United States. Quite a few of them still fly regularly. There is nothing quite like the sound of a Mustang as it passes overhead—the purr of its Packard V-1650 Merlin engine, the low bass of the atmosphere crowding into its distinctive belly scoop, and the faint high whistle through the fighter's machine-gun ports.

Some antique P-51s do more than simply fly. Stripped, chopped, and hot-rodded to the point of lunacy, a handful of these Mustangs are among the fastest piston-powered airplanes in the world. The dangerous and high-priced world of air racing, touted as "the world's fastest motor sport," has found very little that can outrun these venerable veterans of the Second World War.

The Mustang has turned into a legend, an icon, and an emblem of victory in the years since the first of many took to the skies over Southern California. This is the story of the United States' most famous fighter airplane.

Above: One of the prototype Mustangs—the fourth one built—is on exhibit at the Experimental Aircraft Association's AirVenture Museum in Oshkosh, Wisconsin. The airplane holds a place of honor in the museum's Eagle Hangar, astride a runway-shaped ramp that puts the airplane at flying attitude. Note the airplane's two nose-mounted .50-caliber machine guns below its Allison engine. *Zachary Baughman, EAA AirVenture Museum*

Below: In October 1942, US Office of War Information photographer Alfred T. Palmer visited the NAA plant at Inglewood in order to record activities at the factory. Here, Palmer shoots a lineup of Mustang Is and P-51As. Crews put wheels on the center airplane, which appears to have just been painted earlier in the day. *Library of Congress*

SOMETHING FROM NOTHING

IN THE SPRING OF 1940, things looked bleak for the British. After Germany invaded Poland in September of 1939, both France and Britain declared war on the Nazis; Denmark and Norway fell to Hitler in April 1940, and the German invasion of France and the Low Countries began a month later. On May 26, 1940, Allied troops, battered and beaten, began their retreat back to England from the beaches of Dunkirk. Britain, it seemed, was all that was left standing between Hitler and the complete Axis domination of western Europe.

Three days later, the British Purchasing Commission took a gamble on a California-based company to help Britain, in some small way, inch away from the abyss. The organization hoped North American Aviation, founded in 1928, could follow through on its ambitious claims to make the British a top-rate fighter airplane for their struggling nation—though NAA had never built a fighter before.

Amazingly, the EAA's XP-51 flew again after restoration, from 1976 until 1982. The airplane was pulled from the Smithsonian's collection and awarded to the EAA in 1975. The airplane is perhaps the rarest and definitely the oldest of all Mustang survivors. *EAA via the Museum of Flight Collection*

Above: NAA engineer and artist Allen Algier created this drawing in 1940 depicting a partial cutaway of an RAF Mustang. The airplane in the illustration appears to be loaded down with weaponry, including a pair of .50-calibers in the nose and wings, along with four additional Browning .303s. *Santa Maria Museum of Flight*

Below: An NAA drawing showing a cutaway view of the prototype airplane—the short carburetor scoop, odd-shaped belly intake, and rounded vertical tail are some hints that this was a very early version of the Mustang. Note the placement of the weaponry in the nose and the large cavity holding the radiators aft of the pilot. *Santa Maria Museum of Flight*

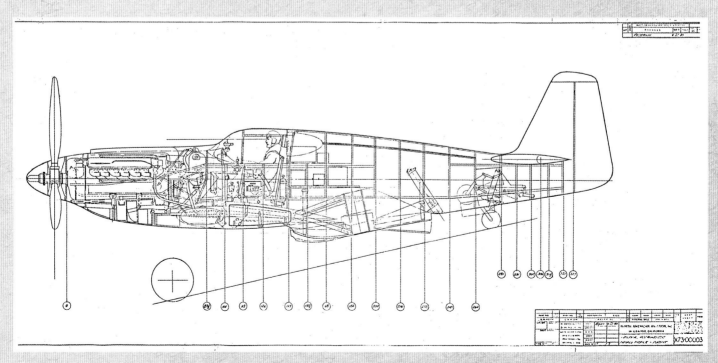

Putting proper grammar aside, they say that if an airplane looks good, it flies good, too. This image shows the clean lines of the NA-73 after it was rebuilt. Note that for some reason, the airplane's striped tail has been touched out of the print. *National Archives*

Every airplane factory in Britain was producing warplanes at maximum capacity. Companies like Supermarine, Hawker, Bristol, and others were pushed to the limit. In the United States, an adjusted version of the US Neutrality Act (1939) allowed the nations of Britain and France to acquire arms from the United States as long as they paid up front, in cash, and hauled the weaponry overseas to Europe aboard their own vessels. Both France and Britain took full advantage of this opportunity, placing orders with nearly every big airplane manufacturer in the United States. Now that France looked as if it would fall within weeks, Britain would take over those orders, too.

One of the standouts in the task of supplying the struggling Allies with warplanes was Curtiss-Wright Corporation, based in Buffalo, New York. It had managed to sell squadrons of Hawk 75 fighters (known to Americans as P-36 Hawks) to France, and some of these would later be diverted to the British for their own use.

At the same time, Curtiss was also swamped with orders for its improved version of the Hawk, which was powered by a big Allison V-12 inline engine; France called this new airplane the Hawk 81A, and Britain called it the Tomahawk. This pair of embattled nations had orders for 1,740 of the airplanes on the books at Curtiss in the spring of 1940. The US Army Air Corps (USAAC) wanted it, too—they called it the P-40 Warhawk, and in 1940, the army ordered nearly four hundred of them. Curtiss was completely overloaded with work.

It wasn't that the P-40 was such a good airplane. Head-to-head against Germany's Messerschmitt Bf 109 or compared to Britain's Supermarine Spitfire, the Warhawk was seemingly a

This Allison ad from July 1941 shows the US Army's "Apache pursuits" before the name Mustang became universal for all fighter versions of the airplane. The artist intentionally warped the image of the fighters to give them a more streamlined look, shrinking the belly scoop, chin, and carburetor inlet on the airplane. *Author's Collection*

full generation behind. It was bigger, slower, heavier, and less powerful than top-of-the-line combat airplanes seen across the Atlantic. Worst of all, it lacked many of the innovations in armor, weaponry, and combat fuel tanks that allowed its European counterparts to survive in battle.

Sometimes, though, the key to winning at war is a numbers game. Though the British knew that the Warhawk was not a world beater, they desperately needed to field thousands of airplanes—decidedly more than they could build on their own. With Curtiss-Wright working beyond capacity, the British Purchasing Commission began a search for an American company that could make additional P-40s under license, and fast.

An obvious choice to mass-produce airplanes was North American Aviation, based in Inglewood, California. The British were already working with NAA to build Harvard trainer airplanes, needed to train thousands of pilots for the war effort. The Allies also showed interest in a new two-engine bomber the company was developing. Now, though NAA had no experience with fighters, negotiations began to create a second source for building the Curtiss-designed P-40.

NAA head James H. "Dutch" Kindelberger knew making the P-40 would be difficult and painful. Time was limited. Examining Curtiss production methods, the engineers at NAA were concerned that they would have to make substantial changes to their typical building processes. Perhaps more importantly, Kindelberger and his team felt they could make a better fighter than the one they were being asked to create. Producing another company's "obsolete" airplane would be immediately lucrative, but the situation seemed to have little long-term value for NAA. As a matter of pride, the designers at NAA were sure that a more aerodynamically efficient airframe, mated with the same type of Allison V-12 used in the P-40, held real promise not only for the Allies but also for the United States *and* the future of their own company.

In days, the designers and engineers at NAA worked to create the preliminary data and first drawings of the airplane that would become the famous Mustang. The British were interested, but they were also concerned about the time it would take to make an entirely new airplane. They could spare only a few months, not a year or more. Republic's P-47 Thunderbolt had been flown for the first time in just under a year. The Lockheed P-38 Lightning fighter had taken almost two years to develop. The idea of creating a top-rate fighter airplane in a few months was incredibly daunting.

AMERICA'S FINEST PLANES

P51 North American Mustang,
Army pursuit plane. Powered
by one 1150-h.p. motor, with
top speed over 400 m.p.h.

America's
finest bread

Bond
VITAMIN-ENRICHED

VITAMIN-ENRICHED
for better health

Above: You can use an image of a sleek Mustang fighter airplane to sell just about anything. Here, East Coast–based General Baking Company's Bond brand bread touts the "P51" as part of its America's Finest Planes series of collectable ink-blotter papers. *Author's Collection*

Right: If it's good enough for our fighter pilots overseas, it has to work well in your jalopy back home, right? Champion artfully melds themes of wartime with the new demands of the home front in its advertisement featuring a hand-scribed Mustang taking on German attackers. Champion spark plugs are still used in many vintage Mustangs more than seventy years later. *Author's Collection*

Far right: Even today, some would argue, "oil is ammunition." Quaker State shows an overturned Nazi staff car and discarded German helmet in the foreground as Mustangs streak overhead somewhere in Holland. The unusual paint scheme may give modelers pause, as will the six machine guns, not seen on a Mustang until slightly later in the war. *Author's Collection*

CHAMPION
SPARK PLUGS have a heritage
established by world speed records on land, water and in the air, gained over many years past, which makes them right at home in our fastest fighter planes. Because of their unfailing dependability in life or death situations, Champions are daily gaining new prestige with the men of our air forces.

Our fighter pilots are writing fabulous history. Legendary feats are being reported daily from all combat areas. Their planes are without equal in performance, maneuverability and speed, and they know how to use these qualities to the limit. Champion Spark Plugs play their vital part in many of these planes. True to their tradition, Champions combine the utmost in performance and dependability in aircraft spark plugs as in those for your car. Now that your car has been "slowed down to a walk" by gas rationing and the thirty-five mile per hour speed limit, all spark plugs need frequent cleaning. At these speeds the heat of combustion will not burn off carbon and oily deposits as readily as at former higher speeds. Fouled spark plugs waste gas, and cause rough, unsatisfactory engine performance. For maximum economy and dependability, have your Champion dealer check and clean your spark plugs at regular intervals.

GET MORE MILES PER COUPON
A B C

CHAMPION
SPARK PLUGS

KEEP 'EM FLYING — BUY WAR BONDS AND STAMPS

The Mustang That Feeds on Oil

WHEN this proud steed and its intrepid "rider" come pounding out of the sky, men of the Axis jump for cover. For it's fast, this North American P-51—and furious.

Fast and furious, too, is the way it drinks oil. Naturally, high-spirited, high-compression motors like that in the Mustang must have not only *enough* oil, but the *best* oil. Indeed, wherever fighting men's lives depend on their motors, these motors must have superlative lubrication.

Fortunately, our side *has* such an oil—and the Axis *hasn't*.

From deep under the good soil of Pennsylvania comes the finest crude oil obtainable anywhere in the world. At Quaker State's four great modern refineries, this oil is given the benefit of a half century's experience in processing lubricants unexcelled in quality.

The Axis has no synthetic lubricant, no oil from plundered wells, that will stand up under grueling war conditions as faithfully or as long as oils with that "Pennsylvania Plus."

For *your* car, too, it's more important than ever to provide the finest lubricants you can obtain. Remember, driving your car *less* does not remove the necessity for expert care in selection and use of motor oil and lubricants. So, where you see the familiar green-and-white service sign, stop for Quaker State Motor Oil and Quaker State Superfine Lubricants— Quaker State Oil Refining Corporation, Oil City, Pennsylvania.

QUAKER STATE MOTOR OIL
CERTIFIED GUARANTEED

Retail price 35¢ per quart

OIL IS AMMUNITION—USE IT WISELY

The XP-46 never delivered on its promise to compete with the Spitfire and Bf 109. It was sluggish, heavy, and more than a little bit ugly. However, the designers at NAA learned lessons from the failed design and incorporated some of the airplane's best traits into their Mustang. The image shows the XP-46A—the second and last XP-46 built. *Santa Maria Museum of Flight*

"We can make a better plane," Kindelberger simply stated to the British. It would take four months for NAA to gear up to make the P-40s. Kindelberger assured the members of the British Purchasing Commission that he and his team could make the new, better fighter—from initial drawings to first flight—just as quickly. It was a bold promise.

The British were impressed enough with the preliminary drawings and projected performance data, and gave the go-ahead to Kindelberger and his team. The British Purchasing Commission put its money on the line soon after and ordered 320 of the airplanes on May 29, 1940. After that, the lights hardly ever went out in the upper offices of the NAA building in Inglewood. Designers and builders worked day and night and into the weekends to create their new fighter throughout the summer of 1940.

The first airplane would be called the NA-73X. The US Army allowed the order with the British to stand under the proviso that they received a pair of the first airplanes off the production line for evaluation. These airplanes, the fourth and tenth from the NA-73 production line, would be designated XP-51s.

Looking to save time wherever possible, NAA wasn't afraid to look elsewhere for data that could help them build their new airplane. In order to appease the British, who simply wanted more P-40s, Kindelberger arranged to access Curtiss-Wright's data on the P-40 and the information on an improved version of the airplane, designated the XP-46. He paid Curtiss $56,000 for the reports and drawings.

The team at NAA was not impressed with them. The first thing that struck them was that the XP-46 was destined to be a

Mustang I (AM190) was retained by NAA for the experimental installation of 20mm cannons. Small numbers of the heavily armed Mustangs went to Britain and the United States, but most P-51s flew with four, then six, .50-caliber machine guns. Though seen in USAAF insignia in this photo, the airplane was eventually released from its testing regimen and served in England with the Royal Air Force (RAF). *Flying Heritage Collection*

hideous-looking machine. Digging deeper and evaluating the airplane's wind-tunnel tests buoyed the hopes of the last of the doubters at NAA—there was little question that they could design something better. One aspect of the XP-46 layout, however, was quite helpful to the designers at NAA: Curtiss draftsmen had been fighting to enclose that same Allison V-12 engine in the nose of their airplane while inducing as little drag as possible. The NAA designers took notice. Particularly intriguing was the aft location of the XP-46's radiator, allowing for a smoother, simpler forward section of the airplane.

NAA designers would argue in later years that the concept of this radiator placement and its possible effects on the efficiency of high-performance airplanes was not a secret held only by Curtiss and that, in fact, the idea was becoming well known to the aeronautics community at the time.

Nevertheless, Kindelberger's team got a look at Curtiss's take on the concept at just the right time to use a similar arrangement in the NA-73.

Additional data came from the National Advisory Committee for Aeronautics (NACA), a US government agency for aeronautic research. Of particular interest to the designers at NAA was NACA's development of new airfoils that could be used in the creation of the Mustang's wings.

Seen from above, the Mustang's wings were simple— almost entirely straight lines with a chord starting at 104 inches and tapering to fifty inches at the wingtips. There was no time for a complex elliptical or semielliptical wing plan like what was used on the Spitfire or the P-47. Seen in cross section, however, the wings were revolutionary. NACA provided NAA with unpublished studies on laminar-flow airfoils, which

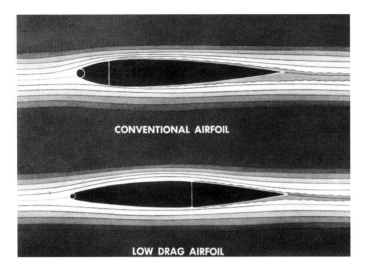

NAA, proud of its laminar-flow wing section, often used drawings like this one in company publications that discussed the Mustang. Moving the thickest part of the wing's chord aft, the passing air adhered to the wing surface a little longer, causing less turbulence and allowing the fighter to be more efficient, so the Mustang could fly farther and faster than many of its contemporaries. *The Museum of Flight*

NAA engineering test pilot Lewis Waite (left) shows off the one-quarter-scale mahogany NA-73 wind tunnel model at the California Institute of Technology in Pasadena in late June 1940. Testing took place throughout most of July. Note the removable light-colored scoop located above the propeller spinner, which was interchangeable with other shapes as NAA looked to create the most efficient design. *The Museum of Flight*

would shift the widest part of the chord aft as far as possible, encouraging adhesion of boundary-layer air for a few more fractions of a second. This would reduce the amount of turbulence when the air separated from the wing surface. If these airfoils worked, the new wings would be amazingly efficient.

However, no one was completely sure the laminar-flow wings would function as advertised. As a result, NAA created a backup plan for the airplane: a more conventional airfoil worked into the exact same wing dimensions, as seen from above. It took testing at the California Institute of Technology, and later at the bigger wind tunnel at the University of Washington in Seattle, to prove that the wings scribed for the NA-73 would be the most efficient of their kind ever created. This single factor is perhaps most responsible for the Mustang becoming one of the most long-ranged and effective fighter airplanes of the war.

The lines of the Mustang's fuselage were just as basic as the wings. Airflow "likes" simple second-degree curves, NAA designer Edgar Schmued explained in interviews after the war, and there was no doubt that the men and women who would be building the airplanes on the floor of NAA's factories appreciated these basic shapes as well. The simple design allowed them to make up to thirty Mustangs a day at the height of production. Front to back, the NA-73's engine was tightly packed into a smooth cowling; only the airplane's top-mounted carburetor scoop interrupted the flowing lines. The entire fuselage was created as narrow as possible, with the cockpit integrated into the clean shape.

One of the most noticeable physical characteristics, of course, was the Mustang's radiator scoop, situated under the wings in the aft part of the fuselage. Since scoops of this type tend to "spill" air and cause turbulence, NAA designers considered this aft location of the radiator optimal for peak aerodynamic performance, as it kept the scoop-disturbed air away from critical areas of the fuselage and wings. Contained in the scoop were the airplane's water-cooling radiator, oil cooler, and aftercooler. Through careful and clever design, this drag-inducing necessity was transformed into a thrust-producing tool.

A British engineer, F. W. Meredith, created a study in 1936 that examined ways to offset the drag created by the scoop, and designers at NAA took full advantage of what was dubbed the "Meredith effect": Air entering the scoop meets the front surface of the radiator(s) and is compressed. Then the air passes through the radiator(s) and becomes heated, increasing the pressure even more. Designers worked to capture the

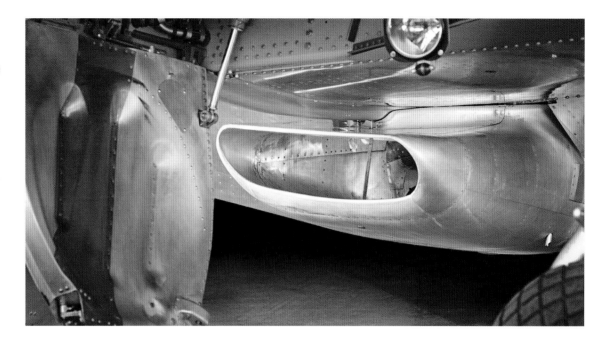

Right: Perhaps the most recognizable part of the whole Mustang airframe is the fighter's distinctive belly scoop. Separated just slightly from the bottom of the airplane, the scoop guides fresh, cold air through the P-51's oil cooler, radiator, and aftercooler. NAA designers shaped the scoop so that the air flowing through it created a small amount of thrust. *Heath Moffatt Photography/Flying Heritage Collection*

energy of the high-pressure air as it moved through the back end of the duct by making the duct narrow toward the duct outlet. Harnessing the resulting thrust helped offset a portion of the drag caused by the intrusive (but necessary) scoop affixed to the bottom of the airplane.

The main landing gear of the NA-73 would be set at a wide stance—there would be almost twelve feet between the tires when the gear was extended on the big fighter airplane. It was a far cry from the notoriously hard-to-handle Supermarine Spitfire (five feet eight inches) or the downright-dangerous Messerschmitt Bf 109 (six feet six inches). The stable Mustang would even have a better spread than the P-40 Warhawk's gear, which stood at eight feet two inches.

It took 2,800 intricate drawings and 41,880 engineering man-hours to create the NA-73X, along with thousands more hours on the factory floor. The designers and NAA's Experimental Department were shooting to finish the project in 100 days—they barely missed their deadline, finishing in 102. On September 9, 1940, the first of thousands of Mustangs was rolled from the factory for a photo session. Never mind that parts of the airplane's brakes and wheels had not met the same deadline. The shots show the new fighter sporting a pair of tires stolen from a production AT-6 Texan trainer.

The shots taken that day became a motivator to correct another, bigger problem facing the Mustang team: they had no engine. Allison V-12s were in high demand, being the engines used in many of the US Army's airplanes—the P-38, P-39, and P-40 fighters. The Allison people figured that no one could

A pilot poses in the cockpit of a P-51A (43-6055). Behind him is the airplane's hard-faced armor plate. As can be seen from this image, peering over the nose of a "tail-dragger" airplane was a challenge while taxiing. Pilots would commonly zigzag back and forth or enlist the help of ground crewmen to make sure they were maneuvering safely. *Santa Maria Museum of Flight*

This striking high-angle front view of the Mustang shows how NAA designers worked to keep the airplane's fuselage width as narrow as they could. Also seen is the airplane's wide-track landing gear—a clear advantage over airplanes like the Bf 109 and Spitfire. *Heath Moffatt Photography/ Flying Heritage Collection*

A lineup of airplanes shows all of the US Army's fighter/attack fighter types, circa 1942. Front to back are the Bell P-39 Airacobra, NAA A-36 Apache, Curtiss P-40 Warhawk, Republic P-47 Thunderbolt, and twin-engine Lockheed P-38 Lightning. All but the "jug-nosed" P-47 flew with an Allison engine. It is interesting to see how simple and geometric the shape of the Apache/Mustang is when compared to its counterparts. The airplane's simple form made it relatively easy to build. *National Archives*

Parked in front of NAA's Inglewood plant, the prototype Mustang awaits its next flight. The tail, which was crushed in the rollover landing in November of 1940, was subsequently rebuilt. Though never serving with the USAAC, the airplane received a set of red and white stripes on its rudder similar to those seen on US Army airplanes as the time. *Santa Maria Museum of Flight*

In the spring of 1941, a company pilot takes the XP-51 prototype out for a flight over the California coastline. The first Mustangs had many distinctive physical characteristics that were changed in the production models, including carburetor scoop, tail shape, belly intake, and makeup of the forward canopy. *Rockwell International via Robert F. Dorr/Nicholas A. Veronico*

have an entirely new airplane ready in just one hundred days. As a result, they put NAA's request for a 1,150-horsepower Allison V-1710-39 engine on the back burner. Like a ransom note, photos of the finished, bare metal airplane, shining in the sun, were sent to the Allison Division of General Motors in Indianapolis. There was no writing attached, but the underlying message was, "We need your engine. Now."

More than a month later, an NAA mechanic fired up the NA-73X's shiny new Allison for the first time. On October 26, 1940, the NA-73X made its maiden flight. The tests, happily, were uneventful. After eight flights, contract pilot Vance Breese turned the testing duties over to another pilot, Paul Balfour. Balfour's first encounter with the airplane was decidedly more exciting.

After twelve minutes in the air, Balfour pulled up to enter the pattern at Mines Field (current site of Los Angeles International Airport), and the fighter's Allison engine quit cold. Balfour made for a nearby bean field and brought the new fighter in with the landing gear and flaps down. As soon as the wheels hit the soft earth, the airplane whipped over onto its back, briefly trapping the pilot before passersby could dig him out of the crushed cockpit.

Subsequent investigation found that the crash was due to pilot error; Balfour had starved the engine of fuel through improper positioning of the fuel selector switch. All concerned felt sure that the design of the airplane had little to do with the crash, and testing would continue with the second airplane (the first production machine). Showing their confidence in

Above: A few last words before a test flight of the NA-73X. The airplane's N-Number, painted on the bottom of the port wing, was NX19998. This image was taken before the airplane crashed at Mines Field in November 1940. *Santa Maria Museum of Flight*

Below: What a sad sight. The NA-73X came to rest on its back in a freshly plowed bean field just 150 yards from Mines Field. At the time of the crash, the airplane had flown a total of just three hours and twenty minutes. The site of the accident is today part of the grounds of Los Angeles International Airport. *Santa Maria Museum of Flight*

NORTH AMERICAN
NA-73
"Mustang" Interceptor
Equipped with
SOLAR
Exhaust System

SOLAR
ESTABLISHED 1927

Solar Aircraft Company

Main Office and Factory: SAN DIEGO, CALIFORNIA | Eastern Office and Factory: PHILADELPHIA, PENNA.

Famous Airplanes, Solar Equipped · Fourth Advertisement of a series

Left: Solar Aircraft Company nearly lost it all during the Depression years, moving from making its own airplanes to building airplane parts for others. By 1939, Solar had 229 employees. This ad, featuring the NA-73, ran in November 1941, as business began to pick up in a big way. Solar made three hundred thousand exhaust manifolds for military airplanes during World War II and topped out at 5,000 employees. *Author's Collection*

Below: At Renfrew Airfield near Glasgow, Scotland, workers remove the protective covering from Mustangs after their journey across the Atlantic. The airplanes were covered in heavy petroleum derivative called paralketone. While it did the job, it was difficult to remove. This photo was taken in October 1943. *National Archives*

RAF pilot John Hill inspects the cockpit of a Mustang in 1942. At first, many American airplanes had seemingly large cockpits for those pilots who were used to the cramped confines of the Supermarine Spitfire. *Santa Maria Museum of Flight*

what they had seen so far, the British had upped their order to 620 airplanes even before the crash.

The original name of the new airplane was Apache, but the British quickly changed their minds. Instead, they would call the fighter Mustang, and by April of 1941, the first Mustang Mk I had taken to the skies. The British Mustangs would come off the assembly line with many additions. These combat airplanes would have guns, armor, and self-sealing fuel tanks in order to survive in combat over Europe. American Mustangs, too, would require wartime gear be added to the fighters.

In August, representatives of the British Air Commission were on hand to witness the packing and crating of the first

Mustang headed for Europe. Hundreds more would soon follow. Not all of them made it through the treacherous journey to England by sea; at least twenty-five brand-new Mustangs ended their combat careers without firing a shot, sliding into the depths of the Atlantic in the holds of torpedoed cargo ships.

A pair of the first Mustangs to successfully make the crossing was immediately sent to Duxford, England, for evaluation by the Royal Air Force (RAF). With the exception of a few teething pains, the RAF pilots rated the Mustang a winner. It was faster than the Mk V Spitfire in level flight, and, perhaps most dramatically, it could fly twice as far as the Spitfire before turning for home.

Above: Women workers at the NAA plant prepare an RAF Mustang for shipment to Britain. Each airplane was fully assembled and test flown in the United States, as evidenced by the splatters of oil under the cockpit, before being crated up for the long ship journey across the Atlantic Ocean. *Santa Maria Museum of Flight*

Opposite: Cadillac and Allison were both divisions of General Motors. Along with manufacturing Stuart tanks, Cadillac helped build 175 different parts used in Allison engines—including crankshafts, camshafts, connecting rods, and piston rings. *Author's Collection*

Of course, the Mustang was a much bigger airplane than the diminutive Spitfire, and heavier, too. It had a sluggish climb rate compared to the bantam British fighter, and, the RAF pilots noted, the Mustang lost a lot of its best traits as it climbed to altitudes above fifteen thousand feet. Just like the Curtiss P-40 it was built to better, the Mustang's Allison engine could not be reliably linked to a proven supercharger system. Where the air was thick, the Mustang was great. High above, it was a bit of a dog.

As famous author Roger Freeman put it, the RAF prudently worked to use the Mustang at altitudes where it could shine: "It was to become very much a 'downstairs maid.'" Of course, it didn't take a genius to muse about what might happen if you put the proven Rolls-Royce V-12 flying in the Hurricane and Spitfire into the nose of the big, sleek Mustang. Almost right away, Rolls-Royce representatives and the RAF set upon the Mustang, hoping to inspire a transplant that would make a good airplane into a great one.

Cadillac

Forty years of "*know how*" in its nose!

Before any of these pilots were born, Cadillac was acquiring a "know how" in manufacturing which will, we feel sure, stand many of them in good stead today.

For one of the wartime jobs entrusted to Cadillac craftsmen is the production of basic power-producing assemblies for America's most famed liquid-cooled aircraft engines. There's forty years of "know how" in the nose of every fighter plane so powered — forty years

that help to endow each with a degree of dependability which only the utmost in precision manufacturing and craftsmanship can insure.

Thus the Cadillac peacetime traditions are carried on in time of war, with this far broader implication—

Cadillac's responsibility today is to nations as a whole—to all Americans—to our Allies—with the clear mandate to produce

vital war materiel in necessary quantities until the need ceases to exist.

Cadillac proudly accepts this trust and is now engaged in war production to the fullest extent in its history. The M-5 light tank, built in its entirety in Cadillac plants, special machinery for the Navy, and other subcontracted war materiel are and will continue to be our sole concern until Victory is won.

CADILLAC MOTOR CAR DIVISION   GENERAL MOTORS CORPORATION

LET YOUR DOLLARS WORK, TOO—
BUY
WAR BONDS AND STAMPS

THE MUSTANG'S FIRST COMBAT

Above left: NAA's Skyline magazine featured what appeared to be a British Mustang I on the cover of its March 1942 issue. AG345, however, never made it overseas. The first production Mustang I had no weapons installed and was kept by the company for testing, production development, and to fix a multitude of small problems, called "squawks" by pilots. *Santa Maria Museum of Flight*

Above right: Get it? It's a play on the American fighter's name. While the US Army waffled, the British were the advocates of the name "Mustang," and the airplane itself, since the very beginning. This simple black-and-white ad ran in US magazines before Pearl Harbor. *Author's Collection*

Due to the Mustang's lack of performance at high altitudes, many of the first RAF versions of the fighter were used for low-altitude missions. Assigned to RAF Army Cooperation Command units, the Mustangs at first had no ground forces to support in operations on the hostile side of the English Channel. As a result, they were used in tactical reconnaissance, with an F24 camera installed behind the pilot's seat to shoot obliquely at ground targets as the planes swept by just a few hundred feet above the ground. The fighters were not only equipped with cameras; they were fully armed and ready to engage enemy forces. As London's *Daily Sketch* put it, "One day it shoots pictures, the next day it shoots German troops."

In January 1942, 26 Squadron became the first to receive Mustang Is. The first of these airplanes to fire its guns in combat was AG418, flown on May 10, 1942, by Flight Officer G. N. Dawson. On that day, Dawson's job involved a low-level photo run over Berck airfield in France. During the pass, Dawson observed and photographed vehicles and suspicious packing cases. He fired his weapons at parked airplanes and hangars on the southeast corner of the field before being chased away by a vigorous volley of small antiaircraft fire and machine-gun bullets. Nearby, Dawson shot up a supply train at La Fesnesie as he left the area.

The first Mustang lost in combat was AG415, flown by Pilot Officer H. Taylor on July 14, 1942. His Mustang is believed to have struck a supply barge he was strafing near Le Touquet.

After August 19, 1942, when British army forces came ashore at the German-occupied port of Dieppe, France, multiple Mustang squadrons worked in concert with ground forces at very low altitudes. As a result, more than a dozen Mustangs were hit and damaged, with at least nine lost in combat activities. It was this day that the Mustang achieved its first out of almost six thousand air-to-air victories of the war—scored by an RAF recon Mustang, serving with a Canadian squadron, flown by American pilot. Hollis H. Hills hailed from South Pasadena, California—not too far from where his Mustang was built.

The first airplane (AL958) of the second group of Mustang I airplanes ordered by the RAF stayed in California for flight-development tests. The fighter sported an odd mixture of a British camouflage pattern with US insignia over the top of its roundels. The airplane was eventually released to combat operations in Europe and served throughout World War II. *Rockwell International via Robert F. Dorr/Nicholas A. Veronico*

A 20mm-armed Mustang IA photographed between recon missions. Note that the airplane has a Spitfire-style rearview mirror mounted above the windscreen and a circular hole cut in the canopy Perspex behind the pilot for the lens of its F24 reconnaissance camera. *Flying Heritage Collection*

Hills and his flight leader, Flight Lieutenant Fred Clarke, were shooting up a German armored column west of Dieppe when a pair of Focke-Wulf Fw 190s appeared. Hills tried to warn Clarke as the Nazi fighters moved in for the kill, but Clarke's radio was malfunctioning, and he was too busy watching developments on the ground to notice. The 190s got to him fast, racking his airplane with gunfire. Clarke bravely turned toward the water, not wanting the Germans to get a look at his sieved but fairly new-to-service Mustang fighter airplane. As he struggled to keep the wounded fighter aloft, Hills was able to pick off one of Clarke's pursuers, earning the first air-to-air victory for the Mustang.

Clarke, too, survived the encounter, though he became the first of many pilots to find that the Mustang's big belly scoop made it almost impossible to land in the water. He violently bashed his head on the gunsight and happily related to an interviewer some fifty years later, "The [shards of] Perspex were coming out of my forehead up until ten or fifteen years ago."

RAF pilots were pleased by the speed and durability of their new recon fighter, which they rated "sensationally fast." On one occasion, a Mustang pilot got in a little over his head near the French coast and had to retreat from a pair of aggressive Messerschmitt Me 110 fighters. Pouring on the coals, he headed for the English Channel, rapidly scooting

Another shot of AG345 in flight over the Los Angeles area. The fighter flew for the first time on April 23, 1941. Retained by NAA, the airplane was tinkered with for years before finally being retired from service in the last weeks of 1946. *Rockwell International via Robert F. Dorr/ Nicholas A. Veronico*

Inset: The RAF pilot's brevet, or "wings," features a laurel wreath surrounding the monogram RAF, topped with the king's crown. *Flying Heritage Collection*

Mustangs
Range the Frontiers of Freedom

Just as the frontiers of America grew beneath the flying hooves of the mustangs, so today's frontiers of freedom are guarded by North American Mustangs — swift pursuits named for the hardy strain of American wild ponies.

These fleet, agile fighters, in active service with the RAF, are helping Britain attain complete supremacy in the air.

CURTISS-WRIGHT CORPORATION · *Propeller Division* · CALDWELL, NEW JERSEY

CLIFTON · PITTSBURGH · INDIANAPOLIS · BEAVER

CURTISS *Electric* PROPELLERS

Above: The RAF's recon Mustangs were originally assigned to the Army Co-Operation Command and used for "long-range, low-altitude daylight intrusion." Later, they flew with the Second Tactical Air Force. Quite of few of the Allison-powered Mustangs served through the entire conflict, as the RAF could find no replacement that could do the job better. *Stan Piet Collection*

Opposite: The month that the United States entered the war, Curtiss-Wright ran this ad showing a Battle of Britain–like scene featuring Mustangs getting the drop on a formation of German bombers. Allison-powered Mustangs flew with the Curtiss-built three-bladed prop. *Author's Collection*

out of gun range and then, a minute or two later, fully out of sight. The Me 110s would have to find easier prey than a speedy Mustang.

Other pilots were not as lucky, getting hammered by ground fire or the bullets of German fighter airplanes. However, it soon became apparent that a Mustang could take the punishment and still give a better-than-average chance of survival to the man in the cockpit. Many limped home with bashed wings, ragged control surfaces, and holed skins. To the British, the Mustang was big, it was tough, and for speedy low-level work, it was the best. Many Allison-powered camera airplanes were still in RAF service years later when the war came to a close.

One NAA Aviation technical representative said he always knew how to get treated like a king when he visited an RAF recon unit: he'd say, "I'm here with the Mustangs."

WARHORSE

MEANWHILE, AT THE US ARMY AIR FORCES (USAAF) evaluation facilities at Wright Field in Ohio, the army's first Mustang sat parked behind a hangar, almost completely ignored. In some ways, the low priority in evaluating the airplane was understandable. The Mustang was considered a foreign project, and the US Army had its hands full testing, evaluating, and improving versions of the Lockheed P-38 Lightning, Bell P-39 Airacobra, Curtiss P-40 Warhawk, and other more pressing projects vital to its own interest.

When the Japanese bombed Pearl Harbor in December 1941 and the United States found itself thrust into war, evaluators at Wright Field became a bit more motivated. Upon testing the new offering by NAA, they had the same feeling as the British: the airplane was good near the ground but had its limitations. It was less than acceptable flying above fifteen thousand feet. Moreover, most of the money allotted to

These P-51B airplanes look very similar, but note that the Historic Flight Foundation's Mustang, closest to the camera, has a slightly different tail. The fillet at the leading edge of the vertical stabilizer helps with longitudinal stability. Though the airplane was not built with one, the fighters were often retrofitted in the field. *EAA/Jim Koepnick Photo*

DESIGN

NORTH AMERICAN AVIATION, INC.
INGLEWOOD, CALIFORNIA,

Above: Created in the summer of 1942, this company-made image shows an A-36, with all six guns blazing. Peculiarly, the airplane carries external fuel tanks instead of the bombs that normally hung below the wings of Apaches while in service. *Santa Maria Museum of Flight*

Opposite: This art deco–style NAA ad appeared in magazines in the fall of 1940—just as the Mustang was being prepared to fly for the first time. The image is simple, subtly reinforcing the speedy evolution of the fighter from drawing board to flying machine in just a few short months. *Author's Collection*

purchase fighter airplanes in 1942 had been quickly assigned to new Lightnings, Airacobras, and Warhawks. There was little cash for these new Mustang fighters.

There was still a line item budget available for attack airplanes, however, and certain interested USAAF officials and those at NAA quickly hatched a plan to keep the new airplane viable in army circles. With the addition of dive brakes and bomb racks, the Mustang could be an "attack bomber," able to do its best work close to the ground, where it was most effective.

The terror-inducing impact of Germany's Junkers Ju 87 Stuka dive-bomber over Poland, France, and Russia was fresh in everyone's mind. Knowing this, the US Army ordered five hundred NAA A-36 bombers in April of 1942.

At the same time, they looked at Allison-powered fighters, too, ordering 310 P-51A fighter airplanes in June 1942 (when new money became available for the next fiscal year). NAA officials had hoped for more. Again, the Mustang's high-altitude shortcomings kept a good airplane from

Left: This grouping of airplanes shows early versions of the three main types of airplanes bound for escort duty in Europe. Closest is the twin-engine P-38H Lightning; in the middle, a P-51A Mustang; and above, a P-47D Thunderbolt. These airplanes served with the USAAF School of Applied Tactics near Orlando, Florida. *National Archives*

Below: Headed into the rarified air over occupied Europe, the Mustang needed a boost. Packard was proud to tout the winning ways of "an even *hotter* Mustang." And, at the bottom of the ad, Packard adds another notch to its belt. *Author's Collection*

UP goes the Mustang's ceiling _ _ _ 2 miles higher _ _ _ _

THE BOYS WHO'VE been flying the bullet-like North American Mustang say it's one of the Army's hottest fighters.

Time and again, though heavily outnumbered by the enemy, they've turned in spectacular box scores.

Imagine, then, what these hell-for-leather American fighter pilots are going to do when they get an even *hotter* Mustang—an even *swifter* Mustang—a Mustang they can push upstairs into the thin high air *farther* and *faster* than they ever could before.

And that's exactly what they're going to get!

For this superb plane is now being powered by the Packard-built Rolls-Royce engine, with a new supercharged surprise: *British and Packard engineers have found* a way to skyrocket the Mustang 2 miles higher than its effective fighting ceiling used to be!

Two more miles of blue sky for Mustang pilots to fight in!

To make this possible, Packard has added engines for the Mustang to its mass-production output—another contribution to the finest fighting Air Force flyers in the world.

PACKARD Precision-Built Power

ASK THE MAN WHO OWNS ONE

MUSTANG fighter   WARHAWK fighter   HURRICANE fighter   LANCASTER bomber   MOSQUITO fighter-bomber   NAVY PT boats

Above: This image allows close comparison between a P-51A (43-6006 *Polar Bear*) and a P-51D (44-72483 *Ridge Runner III*). Note the evolution seen in the Mustang breeds, particularly in the nose and canopy areas. Both warbirds, in reasonably stock condition, have raced at Reno. *Nicholas A. Veronico*

Opposite: Allen Algier of NAA's preliminary design group created this oil painting of US Army Mustangs as the company ramped up to make its first production examples. The piece not only graced the cover the NAA's 1940 annual report, the artwork also helped introduce many NAA employees to the new fighter they would be building when they saw it in the company magazine in early 1941. *Santa Maria Museum of Flight*

becoming a great one. Structurally, the Mustang was one of the best airplanes to fly, was simple to build, and had the most modern and efficient airframe available. But, like the Bell P-39 and Curtiss P-40, it had to drag around that anchor of an Allison engine—an engine that was no good at high altitudes.

Like its counterparts across the Atlantic, the US Army and NAA looked to the Merlin V-12 to solve the altitude performance problem with the Mustang. The American version of

the upgraded airplane would fly with a license-built version of the engine produced by the Packard Motor Car Company of Detroit, Michigan, instead of the famous Merlin built for Spitfires and Hurricanes by Rolls-Royce.

Theoretically, the Merlin-powered Mustang and its two-stage supercharger was projected to give a six-hundred-horsepower boost and stay lively and powerful at altitudes up to twenty-two thousand feet and beyond. Moreover, the

North American Aviation, Inc.

(A DELAWARE CORPORATION)

ANNUAL REPORT
TO STOCKHOLDERS
1940

replacement engine would add only about three hundred pounds of weight to the fighter and could be installed with minimal changes to the existing airframe. Now, all that was left was for someone to prove that the new engine package would work as well as advertised. Could a new engine turn the Mustang from an acceptable fighter into a legend?

In the end, the British built their Merlin Mustang first. Mustang Mk X started life as an Allison-powered Mustang I (AL975). The Rolls-Royce engine donated to the endeavor was originally slated to fit into the nose of a Supermarine Spitfire Mk IX. The conversion didn't take much, though the Rolls-Royce engineers chose to build all new mounts for the airplane. The carburetor scoop on the top of the airplane's nose was omitted in favor of a wide, homely looking opening under the fighter's propeller. This opening served as an inlet to feed both the Mustang's supercharger intercooler and its carburetor.

The newly configured fighter took to the skies for the first time on October 13, 1942, with Rolls-Royce's chief test pilot at the controls. The inaugural ride was a whole new experience. The throbbing, rumbling Merlin felt fiercer than the docile Allison, as if the pilot had slid off the back of his horse and now held the wild Mustang only by the tail.

The new arrangement brought unforeseen difficulties as well. The perfectly balanced Mustang, built for an Allison engine, seemed much less stable with this new four-bladed prop and robust powerplant, particularly at high speeds, when the airplane wanted to slip, twist, or roll—it required constant attention. This new breed of Mustang was just unruly enough to be unnerving to the novice pilot but still be reined in and used quite effectively in combat by a good pilot.

Despite its challenges, there was no doubt that the transplant was a vast improvement, and British officials sent their data and favorable opinions to NAA as tests continued. Across the Atlantic, US officials were fitting their own airplane (a P-51A, serial 41-37352) with a Packard Motor Car Company Merlin. Designated XP-51B, this airplane flew for the first time on November 30, 1942.

Above: Many people say that this airframe is the first stateside Mustang to have a Merlin engine installed. Others think the airplane may be an engineless mockup. Some accounts say that the first Merlin went into an airplane that had 20mm guns in the wings. Could this freshly painted machine with stainless exhaust shrouds and very little weight showing on its gear oleos have no engine at all? *Santa Maria Museum of Flight*

Opposite: For a brief moment in time, the US Army favored Apache over Mustang for the name of its new fighter. This ad appeared in May 1941 and shows fighters—with no dive brakes and no guns in the nose—swooping in for the kill. Eventually, the army assigned the Apache name to its attack bomber version of the airplane. *Author's Collection*

NORTH AMERICAN

SKYLINE

January
1943

Above: What if Japan invaded Alaska? This P-51A Mustang (43-6003) was used to experiment with skis in the place of wheels. In the air, the addition of retractable skis didn't much matter in terms of performance. On the ground, the high-powered fighter was a bit hard to manage, especially with no brakes. In the end, it was judged easier to roll or plow airfields, should Mustangs be needed in snowy conditions. *National Archives*

Right: This issue of Model Airplane News has a striking but somewhat confused depiction of a "P-51B." The airplane, sporting long-barreled 20mm cannons and streamlined nose, looks more like an Allison-powered craft. For the USAAF, as this issue was going to the newsstands, many early-model Mustangs had long since been pulled from combat and replaced with newer fighters. *Author's Collection*

Opposite: Artist Reynold Brown created this cover showing the "scourge to Nazi forces" over Europe. Brown, who went on to create many famous movie posters in the postwar period, met his wife at NAA. Fellow artist Mary Louise Tejeda was employed making illustrations for service manuals for the P-51 Mustang and the B-25 Mitchell bomber. *The Museum of Flight*

Before either the British or American airplanes had taken to the skies, the US government bought into the idea of the Merlin-powered Mustang, at least in part, and placed an order for four hundred airplanes in August—nearly six weeks before the first flight of Britain's Mustang Mk X.

Initially, the Americans experienced problems with the cooling system of their Merlin-engined version. However, with favorable reports from Britain and a semisuccessful first flight of its own converted airplane, the US Army was anxious for all-out production of the improved Mustang. Eventually,

more than 3,700 of the type would be built in California as P-51Bs and in Texas as P-51Cs.

The British originally planned to reinstall Merlin engines in every one of their Allison-powered airplanes, but in the end they decided to order additional brand-new Merlin-powered Mustangs instead. And while all 500 Allison-powered A-36 dive-bombers made it through NAA's production line, only 310 of the roughly 1,300 P-51As ordered by the US Army would ever fly. The balance of the US Army order was quickly changed to contracts for new B-model Mustangs.

SKYWAYS

MILITARY ★ CIVIL ★ COMMERCIAL AVIATION ★ DECEMBER, 1943 25¢

30¢ in Canada

Special Section

AMERICAN WAR PLANES

MUSTANG

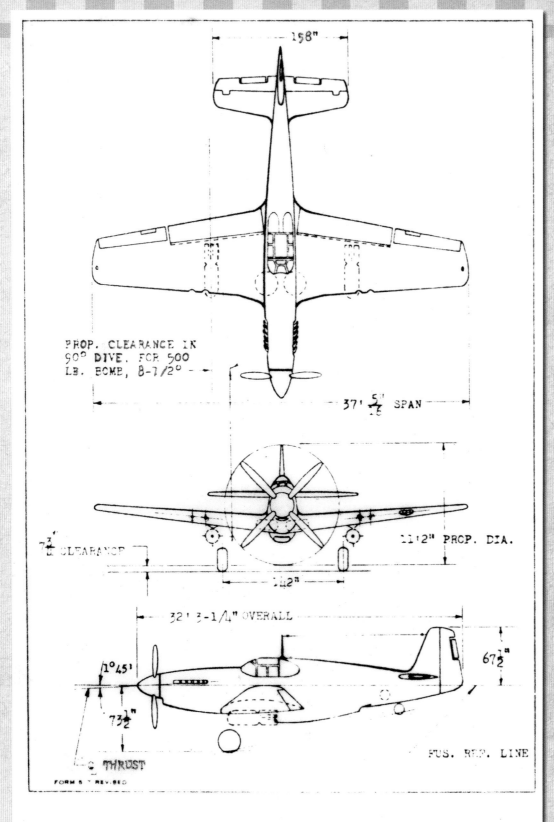

158"

PROP. CLEARANCE IN
90° DIVE. FOR 500
LB. BOMB, 8-7/2°

37' 5⅝" SPAN

11'2" PROP. DIA.

7¾" CLEARANCE

142"

32' 3-1/4" OVERALL

1°45'

67½"

73½"

€ THRUST

FUS. REF. LINE

FORM 5 7 REVISED

P-51B-1-NA

Left: This NAA-produced three-way drawing shows a P-51B Mustang that seems slightly on the chubby side. In those days, of course, there was no such thing as computer-aided design. Engineers had to loft drawings by hand. In this image for the manual, the data on the drawing was more important than the drawing itself. *The Museum of Flight*

Opposite: In 1942, USAAF Capt. Paul Hexter developed an experimental dazzle paint scheme to confuse opponents as to the orientation of the fighter in flight. The scheme, inspired by World War I–era ship paint schemes, was applied to a Mustang IA for tests. While somewhat effective, the paint job was considered too labor-intensive to go into regular service. *The Museum of Flight*

MERLIN POWER

The key to the Mustang's success was its pairing with the Merlin V-12 engine. The famous Merlin got its start in the early 1930s, when Rolls-Royce worked to develop a new powerplant that combined the dependability of its smaller Kestrel with its high-horsepower R seaplane racing engine.

During development, the new engine was called the PV-12 (PV standing for *private venture*). It ran for the first time in 1933. The Merlin was a winner from the beginning, and though developed privately, the engine was used to power some of Britain's most successful RAF warplanes, including the Hawker Hurricane and Supermarine Spitfire. The name Merlin has nothing to do with the wizard of Arthurian legend. Rather, Rolls-Royce named its engines after birds of prey—including Hawk, Falcon, and Eagle. The Merlin is, in fact, a small falcon found in much of the Northern Hemisphere.

There was high demand for the Merlin as Europe entered World War II. Along with the marquee British fighters, Merlins were used in Lancaster bombers and Mosquito fighter-bombers as well. Making the same type of engine for thousands of Mustangs was a challenge that no British manufacturer could tackle during war; instead, Rolls-Royce supplied the United States with two thousand Merlin blueprints and a sample engine, which it delivered to its ally in the hold of a British battleship.

Above: Boise Bee, a Dallas-built P-51C (43-25057), flies near Chino, California. The airplane's paint scheme is that of Idaho native Duane W. Beeson of the 4th Fighter Group. The airplane, restored in 2010, flies with the Warhawk Air Museum in Nampa, Idaho. *Lyle Jansma*

Inset: When the United States needed to pick a company to make Merlin engines stateside, it chose Packard. A luxury-car builder before the war, the company had struggled to sell its expensive automobiles in the financially uncertain times of the late 1930s. *Author's Collection*

Opposite: The idea of a pilot forgetting his engine was a big one during World War II. Packard's ad agency must have been doing its homework. Flying over water or at night, aviators say they hear every strange burble or hiccup in their engines—an early warning that could spell their doom. The idea of forgetting the engine, under any conditions, is truly the "highest compliment." *Author's Collection*

Built to Forget ...that's why it will be long remembered

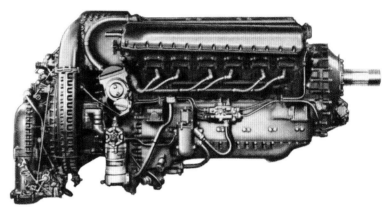

"Built for a pilot to forget!"

That, we believe, is the highest compliment that could be given an aircraft engine.

And that's the reputation the Packard-built Rolls-Royce engine has earned for itself—in famous planes like the Mustang, the Mosquito, and the Lancaster.

Behind the combat record of these Packard-built power-plants is Packard craftsmanship—the ability to turn out precision engines on a mass-production basis, at a rate the enemy never dreamed could be possible.

Packard takes pride in building an engine that pilots can "forget" while they're flying and fighting—but an engine whose role in this war will be long remembered.

ASK THE MAN WHO ~~OWNS~~ *FLIES* ONE

Strafing at ground level or fighting in the stratosphere, pilots bet their lives on Packard-built engines—and win!

 MUSTANG fighter   WARHAWK fighter   HURRICANE fighter   LANCASTER bomber

PACKARD
PRECISION-BUILT POWER

 MOSQUITO fighter-bomber   NAVY PT boat   ARMY rescue boat

• When war progress permits, Packard cars will roll off assembly lines again. They will be cars worth waiting for—built by the same skills that have already produced more than 60,000 Rolls-Royce aircraft engines and Packard marine engines for PT boats.

The American government chose Packard Motor Car Company to make an improved version of the Merlin for US airplanes. British Merlins were built much like Rolls-Royce motorcars—each one was crafted with thousands of handmade parts, making each engine its own "work of art." Packard's V-1650 Merlins would be made in huge batches very quickly, which meant Packard had to engineer parts tolerances in their engines down to 1/100,000 inch or less. The end result was that Packard Merlin parts were interchangeable, allowing for faster repairs and maintenance.

Before each new engine was installed in a Mustang, Packard engineers ran it for six hours at one of its seventy test stands in Detroit. Afterward, the engine was torn down, inspected, reassembled, and run for another five hours before it was sealed in an airtight bag and sent to one of NAA's factories.

Packard made more than 55,500 examples of the V-1650 Merlin during World War II, along with a separate line of marine engines used in patrol torpedo (PT) boats. Not only were Packard Merlins used in Mustangs, but these American-made engines were eventually installed in many Canadian and British-built fighters and bombers as well.

Opposite: Both early-model airplanes in this photograph sport Malcolm Hoods. The bulged canopies, invented for Spitfires, worked to give a fighter pilot a better view than standard canopies. The modification was manufactured by the British firm R. Malcolm and Company. *EAA/Jim Koepnick Photo*

Below: With cowlings pulled for inspection, the Packard V-1650 that powers P-51D (44-72364) *Upapa Epops* can be seen packed into the Mustang's crowded nose. This image clearly shows the scoop and duct under the engine, used to regulate air temperature and pressure to the fighter's carburetor. *Heath Moffatt Photography/Flying Heritage Collection*

Above: Woody's Maytag of the 355th Fighter Group was a California-built P-51B (43-6520). Between missions, the airplane's crew chief dives into the engine compartment to make a few adjustments at its home base, Steeple Morden. Note the airplane's gun ports, taped over to protect the guns from dirt and dust until they could be used in combat. *Nicholas A. Veronico*

Right: This x-ray shot of a Mustang's Packard Merlin, within the nose of the fighter, appeared in an NAA publication near the end of the war. Perhaps the image was the inspiration for the "Invisible Mustang" model made in the 1950s. *The Museum of Flight*

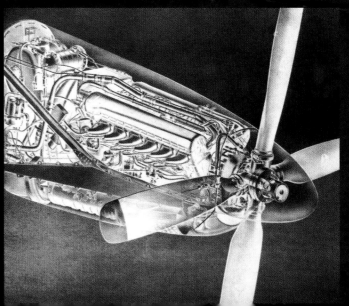

Packard-built Rolls-Royce engines power the Mustang fighter, Mosquito fighter-bomber, and Lancaster heavy bomber. U. S. Navy PT boats and Army rescue boats are powered by Packard super-marine engines. Packard has produced more than 60,000 precision combat engines.

What every motorist can learn from a Mustang pilot

Every Mustang fighter pilot knows this simple truth . . .

. . . that *any* engine — even one built to such exacting standards as the Packard-built Rolls-Royce engine that powers his plane — requires periodic check-ups.

But a lot of motorists have forgotten that fact.

Today, in America, war-weary cars are going off the road, and into the nation's junk heap, at an alarming rate. Thousands of these cars could still be rolling, if their owners had taken just the ordinary precautions that can prolong a car's life.

Don't let *your* car join this "ghost fleet." Go to your Packard dealer and have him check *little* troubles before they grow into *big* ones.

In short, for your own sake, and your country's sake, do everything you can to keep your car rolling. It may be longer than you think before you can buy a new one!

ASK THE MAN WHO OWNS ONE

PACKARD
PRECISION-BUILT POWER

Above: Sometimes, extra priming causes a momentary bit of excitement on startup. Here, right before this P-51D's Merlin catches, sizable flames shoot from the exhaust stacks. The Mustang's flight manual says if a fire develops, "keep cranking engine in an attempt to blow fire out." *Lyle Jansma*

Opposite: A civilian's car is like a Mustang . . . sort of. They both need periodic check-ups or they end up on the scrap pile. The threat of automobiles "giving up the ghost" was a real problem during the war because automobile companies like Packard were building war materials exclusively. *Author's Collection*

While two factories geared up to make the Merlin-powered Mustangs, existing Allison-powered airplanes went to war for the army—a group of thirty-five camera-equipped P-51As were the first to reach North Africa. Just like the RAF's Mustangs, they were fast and performed well low to the ground, making them perfect for tactical reconnaissance. Lieutenant Alfred Schwab Jr. of the 154th Observation Squadron flew the first American Mustang mission over Africa on April 9, 1943, and used the airplane (redesignated an F-6A recon airplane)

to make high-speed runs over a recently captured airfield at Kairouan in Tunisia.

A few weeks after this inaugural mission for the Mustang, the recon airplanes were turned over to another unit, the 111th Tactical Reconnaissance Squadron. After nearly two hundred missions in the area, the only recon Mustang to be lost in combat came when an overanxious American gunner on the ground thought that the angular-looking Mustang was a German Messerschmitt Bf 109 and opened fire. Wide yellow

Top: With dive flaps deployed, a new A-36 sits parked on the ramp at NAA in Inglewood. The airplane has yet to be fitted with its weaponry in its wings or nose. In the background we see another famous dive-bomber of World War II—a Douglas SBD Dauntless. *Santa Maria Museum of Flight*

Inset: Men of the attack and recon units who flew Allison-powered Mustangs in North Africa wore the triangular sleeve insignia of the Twelfth Air Force. It was here that the first of the United States' A-36 and P-51 airplanes went into battle. *Author's Collection*

bands soon appeared on the wings and tails of the Mustangs to give them a more distinctive appearance as they went speeding over the Tunisian countryside.

Next to arrive were units operating A-36 Apache dive-bomber airplanes. The 86th Fighter-Bomber Group was the first in North Africa, followed by the 27th Fighter-Bomber Group, who received A-36s in the place of their Douglas A-20 bombers. In stateside tests, one A-36 had shed its wings in a steep dive, and as a result, top brass in the United States had limited the diving attacks of the airplanes to less than seventy degrees. One official even recommended that ground crews wire the dive brakes of the airplanes permanently closed.

The rules were much different when the airplanes went to combat overseas, where no one listened to safety procedures developed by stateside bureaucrats. In order to land bombs exactly where they were aimed, Apache pilots would dive straight at the ground. Commonly working in groups of twelve, they would find a target and approach from directly overhead from an altitude of 12,000 feet. Dive flaps out,

Above: At a stateside training base, pilots pose with one of their well-used A-36 bombers. The training was difficult, and dive-bombers were always risky airplanes to fly. The Apache had one of the worst records (accidents per hour of flying) of any airplane in the USAAF inventory. *Nicholas A. Veronico*

Left: Near the Anzio beachhead, a dusty P-51 recon airplane pulls in to a revetment made of wine barrels—it is Italy after all! *Betty Jean* probably served with the 154th Reconnaissance Squadron. Note the crewmen hitching a ride to assure that the pilot does not steer the airplane into trouble. *National Archives*

hanging right over their target, the airplanes would scream down one by one at three-hundred-plus miles per hour, dropping their five-hundred-pound bombs while at 3,000 feet and pulling out by the 1,500-foot mark on their altimeter. Friendly troops on the ground were amazed to observe bomb after bomb hitting the same location as the Apaches attacked enemy strongholds.

These "straight in" attacks were quite intimidating to those located squarely in the crosshairs. It is interesting to note that the Germans' much-feared 88mm antiaircraft gun could not elevate to ninety degrees, so once Apaches had moved into position and started their dives, there was little a German gun crew could do to stop them. Enemy soldiers sometimes called the A-36s "Screaming Devils."

American pilots who flew the Apaches considered them "hot ships," fast and maneuverable. Though they were often hauling bombs, the airplanes were a good twenty-five miles per hour faster than the P-40 Warhawk fighters with which they sometimes flew.

However, the A-36 was by no means the top of the aviation food chain in the Mediterranean. German Messerschmitt Bf 109s were still the alpha predators in the region. If pressed, A-36 pilots headed toward the ground and would try to outrun their pursuers if possible—or, once at eight thousand to five thousand feet in altitude, they just might turn and fight. With no bombs, the light and speedy A-36s had the heavy punching power of six .50-caliber guns. Unlike the German Ju 87 Stuka bomber it was designed to emulate, these American attack airplanes could often hold their own once they had shed the weight of their payloads.

The airplanes came on board just in time for the invasion of Sicily in July 1943. That month an NAA technical representative kept a list of the Apache's many victims: 353 motor vehicles, an entire train, twelve locomotives, four large ships, seventeen smaller boats, five airplanes on the ground and three more in the air, seven tanks, seven warehouses, three

Right: Well, it still works! Those flying the Collings Foundation's A-36 couldn't help but put the newly restored airplane's dive brakes to the test . . . from a safe altitude. A small camera affixed to the wingtip of the rare machine records the results. The airplane's dive brakes work in sets, one on the top and one of the bottom of each wing. *Collings Foundation*

Opposite: Six crewmen lift a five-hundred-pound bomb over to the wing pylon of an A-36 named *Robbie* during actions somewhere in the Mediterranean. After the weapon is loaded onto the wing, armorers will affix the bomb's fins and fuses. *National Archives*

Above: Lieutenant Robert Fromm was strafing an ammunition truck when the vehicle violently blew up in front of his speeding A-36. Stunned by the blast, Fromm skidded his Apache through a tree before limping home for a rough landing. The airplane, a veteran of sixty-three missions, was a total loss. "Before the war, I was an undertaker," he joked with reporters. Unfortunately, Fromm was killed in combat in October of 1944. *National Archives*

Opposite: Not all A-36s and P-51As served in Europe. Here, a pilot in Asia ponders the hole left by Japanese ground fire in the wing of his Mustang after a mission over China. Ground fire, not enemy fighters, was the most common threat to Mustang pilots in both the China-Burma-India theater (CBI) and in the Mediterranean. *National Archives*

radar stations, a power plant, a bridge—plus countless docks, buildings, fuel dumps, gun positions, troop concentrations, and more.

Over 2,775 bombs hit enemy materiel in 1,971 A-36 sorties over Sicily. Though the A-36 was officially named the Apache, its pilots during these attacks on Sicily more often than not called the attack airplane the "Invader." Large numbers of A-36s were available for the next large-scale invasion in September of 1943—that of the Italian mainland.

The A-36s soldiered on through the Italian capitulation in September, months of pushing the Germans northward, and

Above: With its dive flaps deployed, the Collings Foundation's A-36 (42-83738) *Baby Carmen* holds steady for the camera. The airplane appears in the colors of the 86th Fighter-Bomber Group. The rare Apache was restored by American Aero Services in Florida and won Warbird Grand Champion at EAA in 2012. *Collings Foundation*

Opposite: While the US Army insisted on the name Apache, pilots and builders seemed to lean heavily on the term "Invader." The moniker was fitting for the tough, fast airplane helping blast Axis armies ahead of the forceful occupation of Sicily and Italy. *Author's Collection*

Previous pages: The ground crew of a 27th Fighter-Bomber Group A-36 Apache proudly pauses for a portrait-style photo with its charge in Gela, Sicily. The airplane, sun-blasted, patched, and muddy, is the veteran of about 140 combat missions. *National Archives*

helping Allied forces hammer through line after defensive line on the march into mainland Europe. In February of 1944, A-36s took part in the much-criticized Allied bombing of Monte Cassino Abbey, which is notable in the fact that many Apache airplanes were overloaded with thousand-pound bombs in order to blast through the walls of the ancient stone monastery.

In less than a year's worth of hard combat from the summer of 1943 through the winter of 1944, the numbers of Apache airplanes that remained operational dwindled dramatically. Though always considered tough, many A-36s returned home with battle damage that could not be fixed. Still more were lost in operational accidents or simply never returned from

flights over enemy territory. By March of 1944, roughly half of the A-36s available to American forces had been destroyed, and a quick phaseout began.

The 27th Fighter-Bomber Group was first in line, turning over its remaining A-36s to the 86th Fighter-Bomber Group and reluctantly transitioning to Curtiss P-40s. The 86th gave up its Apaches in July of 1944 and went on flying combat missions in Italy with Republic P-47 Thunderbolt fighter-bombers. Reconnaissance groups in the Mediterranean flew their Allison-powered Mustangs until new P-51s with Merlin engines arrived to take their place. A new phase in the P-51's history was about to begin.

Yank pilots nicknamed it "Invader"

During the fierce battles for Sicily and Italy, a brilliantly engineered new plane speeded our victory.

Officially known as the A-36, the new North American fighter-bomber was adapted from the famous P-51 Mustang. An American correspondent, reporting on this sensational new ship, cabled:

"The scream of this plane when it dives would shake any man. It makes a Stuka sound like an alley cat.

"When it levels off at the bottom, and lays those bombs right on the target, it zooms away as a heavily-gunned fighter,

looking for Axis troops to strafe, for enemy planes or tanks or trains to destroy. It's a hot ship... plenty fast and plenty rugged. No wonder our jubilant pilots nicknamed it 'Invader.'"

But perhaps more important than its destructive power is the way the Mustang saves lives... the lives of *our* soldiers.

Blast the enemy's planes out of the air ...disrupt his communications...devastate his supply depots and transportation...destroy his offensive power... and you make the task of our ground forces infinitely easier, safer. With air superiority, it's as simple as that.

Through constantly improved designs, and field service on every fighting front, the men and women of North American Aviation are enabled to set the pace in an industry which safeguards America's future. The more and better planes they build, the sooner Axis resistance will be smashed...and the more American lives will be spared.

North American Aviation, Inc., designers and builders of the B-25 Mitchell bomber, AT-6 Texan trainer and the P-51 Mustang fighter (A-36 fighter-bomber). Member of Aircraft War Production Council, Inc.

North American Aviation Sets the Pace!

BUILDING A LEGEND

THE WORKERS AT THREE NAA PLANTS created the most military airplanes of any American company during the World War II years. From July 1, 1940, to August 30, 1945, they built 41,188 bombers, trainers, and fighter airplanes. By way of comparison, during the same time, San Diego–based Consolidated built 30,903 airplanes, and Los Angeles–based Douglas made 30,696.

NAA's massive production volume stemmed mostly from the fact that it designed and produced three airplanes absolutely critical to the war effort: the AT-6 trainer, the B-25 medium bomber, and the P-51 Mustang. The feat is made all the more amazing by the fact that before World War II, NAA had built only small military training and observation airplanes for the US military and a handful of foreign nations.

Before the war, NAA made a living making trainers. Over Tuskegee, Alabama, one of these airplanes makes a flight with the Commemorative Air Force Red Tail Squadron's P-51C (42-103645). The rare Mustang barnstorms the country as part of an educational program, teaching students to rise above obstacles they face in life. *Commemorative Air Force Red Tail Squadron*

In order to complete its first airplane contract, NAA moved from Maryland to sunny California in 1935. There were seventy-five employees working in the company's two-story, ninety-thousand-square-foot factory building on the corner of Imperial Highway and Aviation Boulevard on the border of Mines Field (today within the grounds of Los Angeles International Airport). There, NAA built BT-9 trainers—stout, simple two-seat airplanes used to teach military flying.

Advanced versions of the airplane soon followed, including the one that would become the first in the trio supporting NAA's World War II livelihood—the AT-6. Whereas BT was USAAC code for "basic trainer," the improved airplane, with retractable landing gear and a larger engine, was an "advanced trainer."

The British Purchasing Commission came calling in 1938. Its order for two hundred AT-6-type airplanes, which they called Harvards, helped grow the company immensely. NAA added 1,000 employees in 1938, bringing the total to 3,098. Soon after this first order, the British ordered two hundred more airplanes—and NAA officials knew that in order to have any chance of keeping up, they would have to embrace the idea of mass airplane production.

When Germany invaded Poland in September 1939, the orders increased, including 230 fixed-gear trainers for the French. The Inglewood, California, plant grew by leaps and bounds, from 160,000 square feet in 1936 to 418,000 in 1939 and with 236,000 square feet of additional floor space under construction for 1940.

An experimental medium-weight bomber, first flown in February of 1939, became the second airplane in NAA's World War II trio. Later that year, the USAAC made an initial order of 184 of the airplane they would call the B-25 Mitchell. The Mitchell would be a staple for Allied air forces and would serve en masse with the Americans in North Africa, China, Burma, India, and the Pacific.

In order to keep up, NAA had to expand rapidly. A new facility, intended to make training airplanes exclusively, came under construction in September of 1940 adjacent to Hensley Field Army Reserve Base near Dallas, Texas. Some seventy-five Inglewood-based employees came to direct the

With the control stick tied out of the way, a photographer shoots the cockpit of a P-51D in Inglewood. The white line isolated the six main flight instruments, critical to piloting the airplane. Throttle, propeller, and mixture controls are on the left, and the electrical panel is on the right. *Santa Maria Museum of Flight*

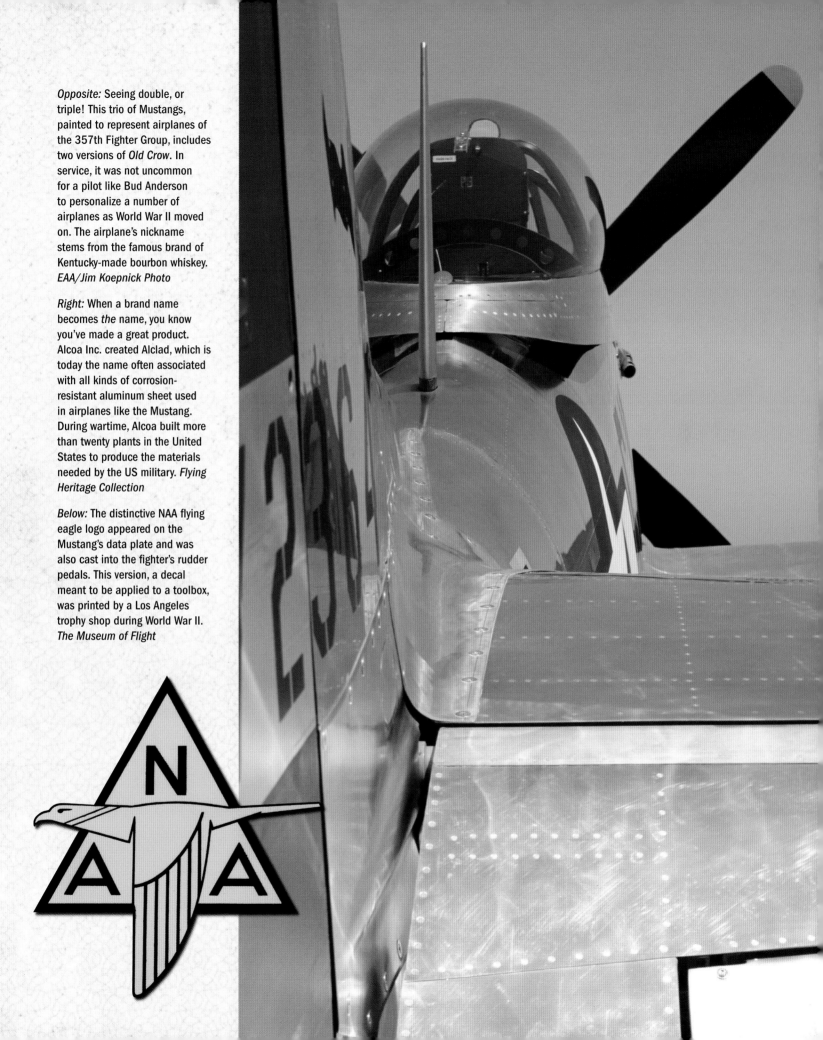

Opposite: Seeing double, or triple! This trio of Mustangs, painted to represent airplanes of the 357th Fighter Group, includes two versions of *Old Crow*. In service, it was not uncommon for a pilot like Bud Anderson to personalize a number of airplanes as World War II moved on. The airplane's nickname stems from the famous brand of Kentucky-made bourbon whiskey. *EAA/Jim Koepnick Photo*

Right: When a brand name becomes *the* name, you know you've made a great product. Alcoa Inc. created Alclad, which is today the name often associated with all kinds of corrosion-resistant aluminum sheet used in airplanes like the Mustang. During wartime, Alcoa built more than twenty plants in the United States to produce the materials needed by the US military. *Flying Heritage Collection*

Below: The distinctive NAA flying eagle logo appeared on the Mustang's data plate and was also cast into the fighter's rudder pedals. This version, a decal meant to be applied to a toolbox, was printed by a Los Angeles trophy shop during World War II. *The Museum of Flight*

Above: Poised to douse the airplane with fire retardant, a ground crewman stands at the ready as the Merlin engine on a P-51B rumbles to life at Mines Field. The fighter's propeller is more than eleven feet in diameter. As Mustang production ramped up, company officials created a mobile metal railing to protect ground crews from the whirling prop during engine run-ups. *Stan Piet Collection*

Opposite: This exploded view is an engineering item breakdown for the P-51D. Of special note is the fuselage fuel cell, number 46. The eighty-five-gallon tank threw off the weight and balance of the airplane. After the external tanks were gone, P-51 pilots did their best to reduce the fuel in this tank before doing any maneuvering in combat. *Santa Maria Museum of Flight*

native Texans, the majority of whom had no airplane-building experience.

On December 7, 1940, a year before the bombing of Pearl Harbor, the US government announced plans for another airplane factory in Kansas City, Kansas. This facility would be run by NAA and make B-25 Mitchell airplanes for the US Army and a patrol bomber version, designated PBJ, for the US Navy.

The Inglewood NAA factory continued to expand as well. By January of 1941, it was just over one million square feet and still constantly growing. Until the Dallas and Kansas City factories were up and running, the California plant would have to handle

a more than $225 million backlog of warplane orders, all needed "yesterday" by France, England, and the United States.

A significant part of that backlog consisted of the growing orders for the third airplane type in NAA's trio—the Mustang. At first, the British wanted 320. Then it was 300 more. In mid-1941, the USAAF ordered 150 more Mustangs, which would be furnished to the British under the Defense Air Program. In the months leading up to America's entry into the war, the workload at NAA was frenzied.

The battle for factory space had been fought and won before America entered the war. Dallas was up and running,

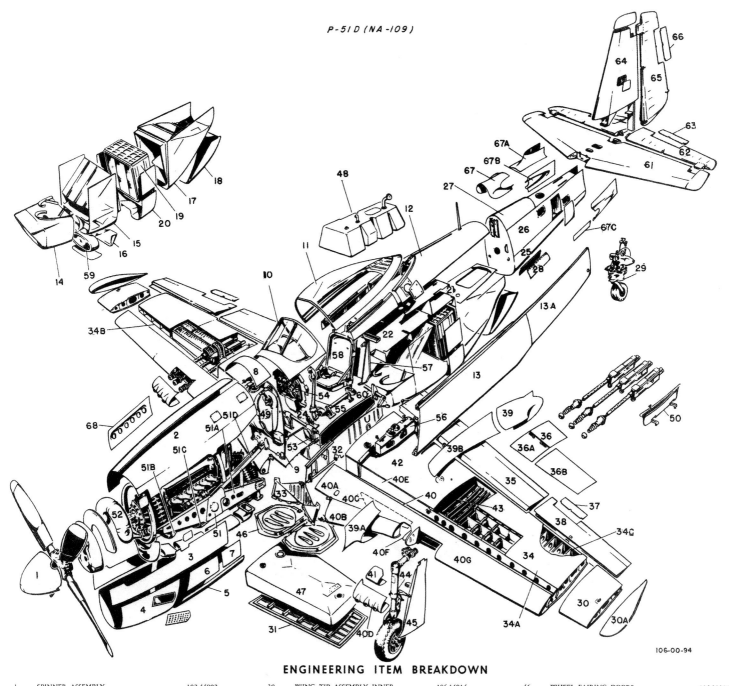

ENGINEERING ITEM BREAKDOWN

1	SPINNER ASSEMBLY	102-44002	30	WING TIP ASSEMBLY INNER	106-14014	46	WHEEL FAIRING DOORS	106-33301
2	ENGINE TOP COWL	106-31573	30A	WING TIP ASSEMBLY OUTER	106-14018	47	FUEL CELL (WING)	102-47002-15
3	ENGINE INTER. COWL	102-31071	31	FUEL TANK DOOR	102-14060	48	FUEL CELL (FUSELAGE)	106-48005
4	ENGINE BOTTOM COWL, FWD.	104-310285	32	WING RIB, STA. "O"	106-14300	49	OIL TANK	102-47002-15
5	ENGINE BOTTOM COWL, AFT.	106-31598	33	WING CENTER BULKHEAD	106-10015	50	WING BOMB RACK	97-63002-5
6	ENGINE INTER. COWL, CENTER	106-31555	34	WING TRAILING EDGE ASSEMBLY	106-14701	51	ENGINE MOUNT ASSEMBLY	102-31901
7	ENGINE INTER. COWL, REAR	106-31599	34A	UPPER INTER. OUTBOARD SKIN	106-14035	51A	MAIN BEAM	102-31902
8	COVER, FIREWALL TO WINDSHIELD	106-310127	34B	LOWER INTER. OUTBOARD SKIN	106-14038	51B	FRONT FRAME	102-31909
9	FIREWALL ASSEMBLY	106-31102	34C	WING REAR SPAR	106-14005	51C	CANTED FRAME	102-31996
10	WINDSHIELD ASSEMBLY	106-318226	35	WING FL	73-18001	51D	BRACE	102-31948
11	CANOPY	106-318251	36	GUN BAY DOOR REAR	106-14052	52	COOLANT HEADER TANK	104-46008
12	FUSELAGE TOP DECK	106-31128	36A	GUN BAY DOOR FWD.	106-14050	53	RUDDER PEDAL ASSEMBLY	99-52403-10
13	FUSELAGE SIDE PANEL, FWD.	106-31107-52 & -53	36B	AMMUNITION BAY DOOR	106-14051	54	INSTRUMENT PANEL	106-51005
13A	FUSELAGE SIDE PANEL, AFT.	106-31107-50 & -51	37	AILERON TRIM TAB ASSEMBLY	97-16003	55	CONTROL COLUMN	102-52111-2
14	RADIATOR AIR SCOOP, FWD.	106-310119	38	AILERON ASSEMBLY	104-16001	56	PEDESTAL ASSEMBLY	106-52506
15	RADIATOR AIR DUCT, FWD.	102-31016	39	WING FILLET REAR	106-10007	57	REAR ARMOR PLATE	106-73520
16	AIR COOLER OUTLET DOOR	102-31023	39A	WING FILLET FWD.	106-10005	58	SEAT ASSEMBLY	106-53009
17	AFT AIR DUCT	102-31079	39B	WING FILLET INTERM.	106-10006	59	OIL COOLER	102-47006
18	RADIATOR OUTLET DOOR	102-31025	40	WING LEADING EDGE	106-14030	60	FLAP TORQUE TUBE	104-52608-2
19	RADIATOR ASSEMBLY	102-46005	40A	TOP FWD. INBOARD SKIN	106-14033	61	HORIZONTAL STABILIZER	73-21001-100
20	RADIATOR BOTTOM COVER	102-310106	40B	AUXILIARY NOSE ASSEMBLY	106-14040	62	ELEVATOR	73-22001
21	FUSELAGE AFT SHEAR WEB	102-31202	40C	LOWER FWD. INBOARD SKIN	106-14036	63	ELEVATOR TRIM TAB	97-22003
22	FIXED RADIO SHELF	106-31205	40D	GUN NOSE ASSEMBLY	106-14029	64	VERTICAL STABILIZER	73-23001
23	TO BE ISSUED WHEN AVAILABLE		40E	FRONT SPAR	106-14004	65	RUDDER	73-24001-40
24	FIXED INSTRUMENT PANEL	106-31137	40F	LANDING GEAR SUPPORT	91-33106-10 & -11	66	RUDDER TRIM TAB	97-24003
25	FUSELAGE REAR SECTION, LOWER	73-31110-200	40G	UPPER OUTBOARD NOSE ASSEMBLY	106-14040	67	EMPENNAGE FILLET FWD.	106-20012
26	FUS. REAR SECT. SIDE PANEL L.H.	97-31026	41	LANDING GEAR ACCESS DOOR	106-14032	67A	FIN FILLET FWD.	106-20013
26A	FUS. REAR SECT. SIDE PANEL R.H.	97-31027	42	UPPER INTERM. INBOARD SKIN	102-14034-100 & -101	67B	STABILIZER FILLET REAR	106-20015
27	FUS. REAR SECT. TOP DECK	106-31116	43	WING STA. 75 RIB ASSEMBLY	106-14802	67C	EMPENNAGE FILLET LOWER	106-20014
28	TAIL WHEEL DOORS	73-31066	44	LANDING GEAR STRUT	73-33102-10 & -11	68	STACK FAIRING	102-42023
29	TAIL WHEEL ASSEMBLY	97-34101	45	STRUT FAIRING	106-33302			106-00-94

NOTE: FOR INSTALLATION DWG. NOS. REFER TO NA DWG. 106-900002

EXPLODED VIEW OF THE AIRPLANE

Above: A Mustang I, bound for England, gets crated for transport early in the war. Beyond the box, parts of the airplane were protected with padded cradles, special wrapping, and slopped with Cosmoline (an oily preservative chemical). Later, airplane companies struggled to come up with a better, quicker way to ship new airplanes. *Santa Maria Museum of Flight*

Right: Early one morning, photographers shoot a lineup of Mustang IIIs bound for RAF service. The equivalent of the P-51B, Mustang IIIs were well liked in England, and British mechanics were able to mildly tinker the engines to allow the airplanes to fly a speedy 417 miles per hour at two thousand feet. *Stan Piet Collection*

Kansas City was very close, and Inglewood had grown to massive proportions. However, NAA needed more than just space to make airplanes. Floor space was the simplest problem to remedy; the factories also needed people, materials, and machinery. At the time, every press, punch, and lathe west of the Mississippi was fervently sought after by Lockheed, Douglas, Consolidated, Vultee, Northrop, Ryan, and others. It was the same for every bit of tubing, electrical wire, and block of aluminum. For the war effort, the West Coast companies put aside their differences, forming the Aircraft War Production Council, which included the seven major California companies, as well as Seattle-based Boeing.

Someone at NAA got the idea that rubber was being wasted as workers moved new Mustangs around in the factory and on the ramp. Could substitute wheels be used in their place? Perhaps more of a PR stunt than actual long-term consideration, the wooden wheels were briefly affixed to an RAF Mustang Mk IA. How embarrassing for the sleek new fighter! *National Archives*

They shared and traded supplies, techniques, and sometimes even people. NAA, one of the richest of the California companies, often seemed to be helping others. The company donated two-inch chrome tubing to Lockheed for its waiting line of P-38 Lightning fighters in addition to turning over data on the B-25's landing gear system to the engineers at Northrop, who were struggling to design the P-61 Black Widow night fighter. However, there were times that NAA gained insight and technological know-how from the other companies, too.

One such instance came up during the redesign of the Mustang, when NAA engineers were converting it from fighter to dive-bomber. They had no experience with building dive flaps, and they turned to Vultee, who had been creating a dive-bomber for the French and British. Quickly, a courier drove an entire set of flap blueprints westward about fifteen miles from Vultee in Downey, California, to Inglewood, giving NAA "a $250,000 gift to the war effort."

Locating aircraft workers was one of the biggest issues that faced the US home front throughout the entire war. Even with massive factory buildings and limitless tools and supplies, not one Mustang could be built and flown on its first test flight without thousands of workers. During the years leading up to the entry of the United States into World War II, the population in California exploded. Thousands of families, black and white, migrated from the South and Midwest seeking jobs after

Above: In dim lighting, Office of War Information photographer Alfred T. Palmer captures the construction of an Allison-powered Mustang in October 1942. The bar between the airplane's main gear assures that it cannot collapse during the production process. Note the intricate leather-covered pilot's seat placed in front of the airplane. *Library of Congress*

Left: The P-51B must have been out of the flightline on a day where someone in the press office said, "Take more pictures." The Mustang with the easy-to-remember serial number of 43-12342 appears in many shots, both in the air and on the ground. Here, a mechanic runs up the engine before test flight. *Nicholas A. Veronico*

Above: A shot taken from the roof of the NAA building reveals scores of B-25J and P-51B airplanes, ready for combat. Among them, airplanes went to Europe, the Pacific, and the CBI. The Mustang under the wing of the RAF B-25 seen in the lower left corner was assigned to the 51st Fighter Group in China. In December 1944, on a ferry flight between Chihkiang and Kunming, the pilot encountered bad weather and ran out of fuel. He was killed in the forced landing. *The Museum of Flight*

Opposite: In May 1944, a new Mustang is loaded into the hold of a cargo ship. Wrapped with a spray-on corrosion-control substance called Plastiphane, the new fighter would be protected until it arrived overseas. This method of transport replaced crating the new airplane. It was cheaper and took up less floor space, allowing for bigger loads. At the Mustang's destination, it took three to four hours to remove the protective material. *National Archives (California Division)*

the Great Depression. The airplane companies in Southern California were eager to supply jobs in great numbers.

Just when NAA seemed to have all of its operational and production problems in hand, the Japanese bombed Pearl Harbor, and the United States officially went to war the next day. With the country engaged in the fight, orders for new airplanes skyrocketed.

NAA made 171 B-25 bombers in 1941. The next year it would produce 1,555, and the year after that 2,953. Fanfare scheduled to accompany the official opening of Kansas City was cancelled hours after the attack on Pearl Harbor, and workers simply concentrated on churning out as many weapons of war as they could. Initial wartime orders for Mustangs included 500 A-36 attack airplanes and 310 P-51As for the US

P-51D (44-72438) *Hell-er Bust* is based in Boise, Idaho. Seen here with two other Mustangs from the Pacific Northwest, the fighter flew with the Eighth Air Force during World War II and was then sold to Sweden. Later the airplane became of part of the Dominican Republic's air force, which flew P-51s into the 1980s. *Hell-er Bust* was restored to World War II configuration in the 1990s. *Lyle Jansma*

Betty Jane, a P-51C (42-103293), flies with the Massachusetts-based Collings Foundation. Collings airplanes travel the country, visiting airshows and giving rides. The airplane not only has room for two, it has a second set of controls, allowing a lucky enthusiast to fly a vintage Mustang! *Collings Foundation*

Army—quite modest interest considering the circumstances. After 223,062 engineering hours and 1,500 drawings, the addition of the Merlin engine to the sleek Mustang airframe opened the floodgates.

Inglewood would produce some 1,990 P-51B Mustangs ordered in 1942 and 1943, and the plant at Dallas built 1,750 P-51Cs. As NAA ramped up production to near-impossible levels, its workforce began to erode heavily—losing young men to military conscription had been an issue since late 1940, but now priorities began to diverge. At one point, NAA leaders told the government flatly to decide whether it wanted more men or more airplanes. By September of 1944, NAA had granted eleven thousand military leaves for employees.

Opposite: Skyline's cover in Sept/Oct 1944 featured a Women's Airforce Service Pilot (WASP) ready to climb into the cockpit of a new Mustang fighter. Strangely, in October 1944, a female Army pilot disappeared while ferrying a P-51 from California to New Jersey. Historians suspect that Gertrude Tomkins Silver's new Mustang crashed in the ocean moments after takeoff from Mines Field. She remains the only WASP to go missing during the war. *Santa Maria Museum of Flight*

Before the war, about 77 percent of a typical California airplane factory could be drafted: those employees who were male, eighteen to forty-five years of age, and physically able. During this time, less than 1 percent of the workforce was made up of women. By the height of production in late 1943, however, nearly 65 percent of airplane industry workers were

NORTH AMERICAN

SKYLINE

SEPTEMBER-OCTOBER
Vol. 5   No. 4   1944

NORTH AMERICAN AVIATION, INC.
PHOTOGRAPHIC DEPARTMENT
INGLEWOOD CALIFORNIA

Above: This glorious panorama shows the Mustang final assembly line at Inglewood, almost beginning to end. Wings are on the left with fuselages coming together nearby. Note the suspended tail and engines being added after the U-turn on the floor. On the right, after the wing join, nearly whole Mustangs get finishing touches as they migrate toward the factory doors. *Santa Maria Museum of Flight*

Left: It is interesting to note that by 1945, when this ad came out, there were just as many women working at NAA than men—probably more. The tagline works off the famous "Keep 'em Flying" motto that had been around since 1941. In order for the army to uphold its end of the bargain, first NAA and others had to put them together. *Santa Maria Museum of Flight*

female. It is no exaggeration to say that wartime P-51s were primarily built by women.

NAA looked elsewhere for labor as combat in North Africa, Europe, and the Pacific took more and more fighting-age men onto the frontlines. Recruiters cruised pool halls and local skid rows for warm bodies. Other workers dropped off parts and projects at convalescent homes. World War I vets were given buckets of hardware swept from the factory floors to sort, rebox, and send back to the factories. NAA estimated that

sorters worked through enough stray nuts and bolts to make five P-51 Mustangs—around nineteen tons of hardware!

The war changed the racial makeup of the workforce at airplane factories as well. Whereas these factories typically employed white workers, now black, Hispanic, and American Indian employees began working alongside white men and women on NAA's airplane-building lines.

Many employees doubled or tripled their workload to make up for the lack of sufficient labor. Stateside-based soldiers came in to factories to build Mustangs and other airplanes part time and then full time when they were on leave from their post. In some cases, high-school and junior-college students went to school for half of the day and worked at the NAA plant for the other half . . . and all day Saturday.

There were certain advantages to having such a varied workforce. Small boys could scramble into the tail of a P-51 to hold a bucking bar while a "Rosie the Riveter" blasted in fasteners from the outside. Deaf workers were assigned jobs in the factory's planishing rooms, where hammers thundered all day long producing Mustang fairings. Blind workers were given the task of assembling push rods, flap hinges, and mounting brackets, as they could consistently put the complex parts together by feel.

The corps of men and women employed on NAA's Mustang lines in California and Texas were working, of course, to make fighters—as many as twenty per day. The company worked hard to ensure nothing else got in the way and provided daycare facilities and nursery schools for employees. Company representatives were present to fix a worker's car, fight an employee's speeding ticket, or provide workers with all they wanted to eat for only fifty cents. Managers brought doctors to the plant to give onsite draft-board physical examinations (thus saving thousands of worker hours) and would dispatch nurses to employees' houses if they called in sick. Nothing was going to stand in the way of producing an endless line of Mustangs.

It is important to note, however, that a Mustang had a whole other life before being joined together on the factory floor. In fact, much of the airplane's production existence was spent in small unrecognizable pieces. "Don't let 'em get too big too soon," was the direction of NAA president Dutch

A pair of NAA products is parked tail to tail in this PR photo of a lady stenciler working outside the Inglewood plant. The airplanes in the background are B-25H Mitchells. The Mustang seen up front is a P-51B bound for Europe. The airplane would be assigned to the 357th Fighter Group. During a flight to Rechlin, Germany, the Mustang experienced engine troubles and the pilot diverted to Sweden, where he crash-landed. *Santa Maria Museum of Flight*

Kindelberger. He had learned this mass-production tactic from automobile companies.

Massive-scale mass production of airplanes was a new concept at the beginning of World War II. Airplane companies had never needed to make so many before, and they looked to automobile manufacturers for hints on how to handle the process. They were told, "Start out with the plane's parts in a thousand different places."

NAA subcontracted these thousands of components that would go into each P-51, and parts were collected from different producers from all over the United States. These parts included aluminum from Alcoa in Pittsburgh, carburetors from Bendix in Maryland, gun-feed motors from Hughes of California, gunsights from Sperry of New York, propellers

This red-tailed beauty flew with the Royal Australian Air Force and various warbird collectors before being damaged in a crash in 1976. The P-51D/CA-18 (A68-39) is owned by Jack Erickson, founder of an Oregon-based aviation company. In order to minimize maintenance, many flying Mustangs are completely painted, in the place of the fighter's original bare metal skins. *Lyle Jansma*

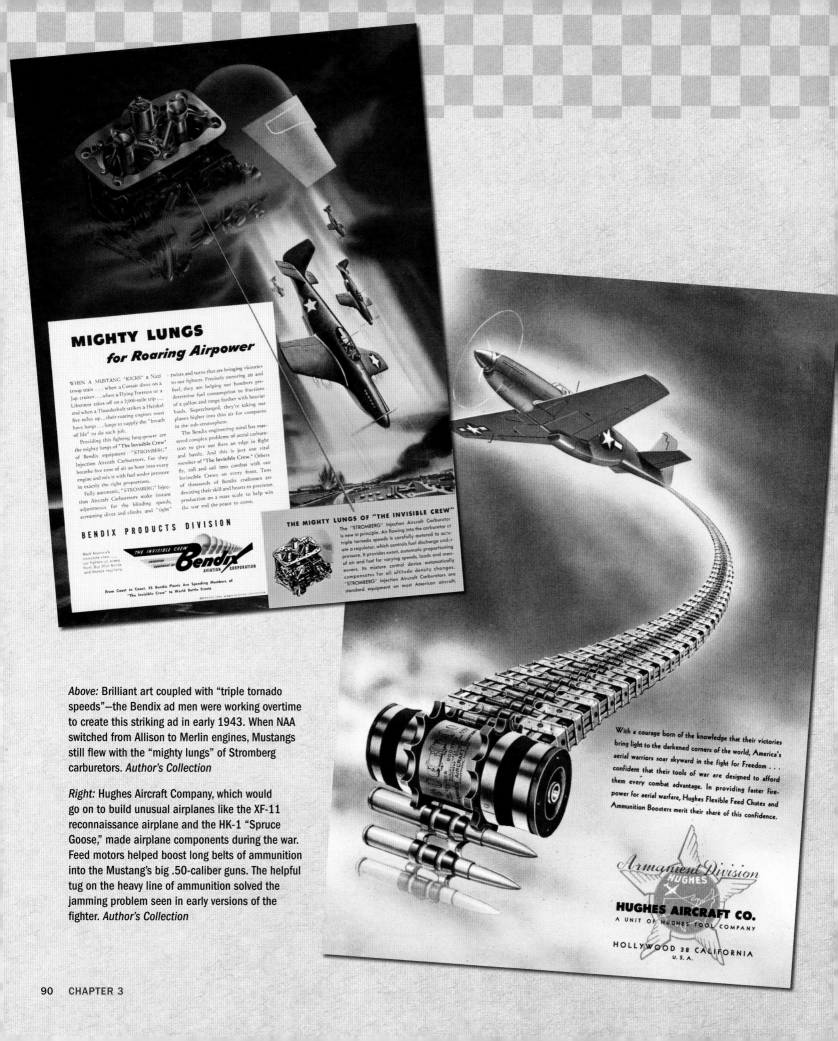

Above: Brilliant art coupled with "triple tornado speeds"—the Bendix ad men were working overtime to create this striking ad in early 1943. When NAA switched from Allison to Merlin engines, Mustangs still flew with the "mighty lungs" of Stromberg carburetors. *Author's Collection*

Right: Hughes Aircraft Company, which would go on to build unusual airplanes like the XF-11 reconnaissance airplane and the HK-1 "Spruce Goose," made airplane components during the war. Feed motors helped boost long belts of ammunition into the Mustang's big .50-caliber guns. The helpful tug on the heavy line of ammunition solved the jamming problem seen in early versions of the fighter. *Author's Collection*

Moonbeam McSwine, a P-51D Mustang (44-73656) sold as surplus in 1958 for $1,307.50. The former Air National Guard (ANG) fighter went on to be reworked by Cavalier and sent to El Salvador. It was brought back to the United States in 1974. Today, the airplane is registered in France. *EAA/Jim Koepnick Photo*

from Hamilton Standard in Connecticut, and engines from Packard in Michigan, to name just a few of the big pieces. Other recognizable companies added to the mix with a myriad of parts—General Motors (radiators), Browning (guns), Goodyear (tires), Firestone (fuel tanks), General Electric and Delco (magnetos), and Pesco (pumps).

This flood of parts arrived at six offsite subassembly plants in the greater Los Angeles area (in the case of Inglewood-bound Mustangs). At these sites, thousands of parts were put together in hundreds of stations within this sextet of miniplants. Here, unskilled people, with lots of elbow room, could put together the thousands of components into

Snifter, a P-51D/CA-18 (A68-110) was sold for scrap in Australia in the 1950s. After years of restoration the airplane emerged in its current state in 2002. Modified to hold two, the airplane attends airshows in Australia and gives visitors down under a chance to ride in a Mustang. *Gavin Conroy*

hundreds of minor parts. Company transports then trucked these assembled parts to Inglewood for larger production.

At the main factory, more stations, also staffed by semi-skilled workers, put together hundreds of pieces into a few major subassemblies and attempted to finish the large sections of airplane down to the last rivet. Fuselage-group employees did not simply get the cockpit "close to done"; they did their best to finish it completely. While there was still a reasonable amount of space to move about, workers put knobs on the throttle handles, belts on the seats, gunsights above the full instrument panels—right down to the signal flare pistol affixed to each bulkhead. Only then did the section leave for final assembly.

The assembly line constantly changed over the course of the war, but in a general sense, crews riveted a nearly fully assembled tail onto a main fuselage section and then moved on to the next airplane in line. Sometimes the crews moved and sometimes the airplanes did, rolling on dollies along the factory floor. Zigzagging over the factory layout, the partly finished Mustangs would be pushed one way and then U-turn to move in the opposite direction as they grew in size. Later, they traveled on their own, rolling while affixed to a motorized rail conveyor system.

Behind the riveting crew—literally and sequentially—another group of workers connected cables and wires leading to the aft end of the fighter. Next, cranes lifted the fuselage onto the one-piece wing, which had been turned up onto its main landing-gear wheels only moments before the connection was made. After the two large pieces were affixed with heavy bolts, employees worked to connect rods, ducts, cables, and wires.

Next came the engine, dropped down into place at the nose of the airplane. Built as a quick engine change (QEC) package, the V-1650 Merlin and its surrounding support pieces bolted into place quickly as the Mustang moved down the line. Almost finished, crews scurried over each one, affixing panels, canopy, cowlings, and other parts intentionally left off until the end in order to allow access to all areas of the airplane. The fighter also received its propeller, hub, and aft spinner, all preassembled and hung into place on the Merlin's drive shaft at once.

At the end of the line, the new Mustang hit sunlight for the first time as it rolled out to the tarmac. (In busy times, it was not uncommon for some of the airplane's assembly process to take place outdoors as well; the weather in Southern California generally cooperated.) The airplanes were also painted outdoors until later in the war when, in order to save time and weight, NAA delivered Mustangs in bare aluminum. Some sixteen pounds of camouflage paint, no longer needed over Europe or the Pacific, actually drained as much as eight miles per hour off the Mustang's top speed and gobbled up a few miles in combat radius.

Engine runs and test flights took place at a breakneck pace as corps of ground crews and test pilots handled twenty or more Mustangs a day. In January of 1945 and again in March

Four NAA crewmen await the arrival of a suspended fuselage to join with a set of wings below. A few big bolts will join the two pieces forever. Unlike in the past, when shop directions might have said "bump to fit" or "file to suit," the virtually endless line of uniform Mustang parts bolted and riveted into place quickly, and nearly seamlessly. *Stan Piet Collection*

GEORGE WELCH

There was a genuine war hero among NAA's corps of test pilots at the Inglewood plant. George Welch was an army flying ace, Medal of Honor nominee, and Pearl Harbor combat vet.

Fellow pilot and ace Francis Gabreski said of Welch, "He was a rich kid, heir to the grape-juice family, and we couldn't figure out why he was there since he probably could have avoided military service altogether if he wanted to." However, Welch decided he wanted to fly and was stationed at Pearl Harbor on the day World War II began for the United States.

On the morning of December 7, 1941, he and another pilot, Kenneth Taylor, took to the skies in their Curtiss P-40 fighters while hundreds of Japanese fighters and bombers prowled the island of Oahu. Welch shot down four attacking airplanes while Taylor claimed two. They were nominated for the Medal of Honor for their actions but reportedly downgraded to receiving Distinguished Service Crosses because they had both taken off without orders. After Pearl Harbor, Welch went on to fly P-39s and then P-38s in combat. He shot down a total of sixteen enemy airplanes before he retired from army service with the rank of major.

In 1944, Welch joined NAA as a test pilot. On a normal day, he would make first flights in some of the many P-51 Mustangs coming off the production line at Inglewood. He would later become chief test pilot of NAA's swept-wing XP-86 jet fighter and made the first flight of that airplane in October 1947. Though never officially acknowledged, there are some who think that Welch may have actually used the XP-86 Sabre to fly faster than the speed of sound, weeks before Chuck Yeager broke the sound barrier in the Bell X-1.

Sadly, Welch was killed while flying for NAA. In 1954, the F-100 Super Sabre he was testing broke apart while pulling out of a dive at more than one and a half times the speed of sound.

NAA test pilots take a break between flights. From the left are Edward Virgin, Robert Chilton, George Krebs, and ace pilot George Welch. It is interesting to note that all of the pilots wear leather wingtips in the cockpit. *Santa Maria Museum of Flight*

Top: A factory scene in California shows P-51D Mustangs under construction. By this time, the airplanes move along the floor, slowly making their way to completion. Note the platform the worker stands on at the right of the photo. His workstation is pulled right along with its assigned fuselage section. *Stan Piet Collection*

Above: A shiny new Dallas-built P-51C ran into trouble on a factory test flight. The Mustang is tough, but you can't use it to jump ditches! Brought back to the factory and quickly repaired, the airplane served throughout World War II and was condemned to salvage in November 1945. *Santa Maria Museum of Flight*

Left: Pilots say that the cockpit of the P-51 had a great layout. Perhaps that was because many of them were used to flying other NAA products. Many novice pilots spent hours of stick time in NAA AT-6–type trainers before moving on to bigger, more powerful fighter airplanes. *Heath Moffatt Photography/Flying Heritage Collection*

of the same year, NAA built more than eight hundred P-51s—more than thirty in one workday!

Changes were happening constantly at all points in the construction process. Most were minor—an additional locking cable spring, an improved type of gunsight, or a new set of rocket launch rails. Other changes were more involved. On the production line, both Dallas and Inglewood switched to building D-model Mustangs in the place of their "razorback"

Left: Ready to go? A Mustang pilot poses with his Dallas-built P-51K. The pilot is truly ready to fly, with parachute, gloves, and throat mic all in place. Note that the gun ports have been covered and sealed for travel. *Santa Maria Museum of Flight*

Below: The first D-model Mustang started life as a P-51B. The tenth P-51B (43-12102) stuck around the factory for some serious modification. Designers tore into the top of the fighter and made their plans for an improved cockpit into a reality. Engineers had tested a "bubble-topped" Mustang in the wind tunnel, but now they could see how the real thing behaved in the air. *Stan Piet Collection*

B- and C-model Mustangs in 1944. The P-51D most notably flew with a large, blown-Plexiglas "bubble" canopy, which offered much better visibility to a combat pilot than B- and C-model aircraft. Additionally, the D model carried two more M2 .50-caliber machine guns, giving the fighter more punch. Other adjustments included slight improvements to the engine, landing gear, cowlings, and control surfaces. In order to fix the Mustang's tendency to snap-roll during slow-speed maneuvers, NAA developed a dorsal fillet that was installed forward of the fighter's vertical stabilizer. The company made kits to refit airplanes already in the field and began incorporating the new part into production airplanes as well.

K-model Mustangs were similar to P-51Ds but had an Aeroproducts propeller in the place of the Hamilton Standard unit. When Hamilton Standard could not keep up with the rate of production, Dallas took on these new props, made by the Aeroproducts division of General Motors in Ohio. Though not liked by pilots as much as the Hamilton Standards, the Aeroproducts kept the Texas facility up and running without delays. It built 1,500 P-51K airplanes.

Inglewood took on building P-51H Mustangs near the end of the war. The H model was a totally new design, meaning nearly everything was different for the men and women on the factory line. It was noticeably different physically, with an improved engine, taller vertical tail, and longer fuselage, and was six hundred pounds lighter than the standard Mustang. The first P-51H flew in February of 1945, though the USAAF had ordered 1,000 of them months before—in June of 1944. Some 370 of them were built in California before Japan's surrender. Dallas, too, was going to switch over to the type, but the war ended before the changeover took place.

The surrender of Japan in August 1945 changed everything at NAA. On August 20, Kindelberger addressed his employees: "The Army Air Forces has cancelled all work hitherto performed at Kansas City and Dallas. [They have also] cancelled more than seventy-five percent of the production previously called for at Inglewood. As a result, nearly twenty-five percent of the P-51H contract, together with some experimental work, remains in force at this plant.

Weekly
SERVICE NEWS
NORTH AMERICAN AVIATION, INC.
FIELD SERVICE DEPT. INGLEWOOD, CALIF.
MAY 28, 1945   VOLUME 3—NUMBER 41

Here It Is—
YOUR
P-51H

Now that the P-51H is winging its way into battle skylanes in real numbers, *Weekly Service News* feels that it's time to have a brief look-see at this latest Mustang to check how it stacks up against its predecessor—the D—and to give you the low-down on what's new and different, about this North American fighter.

But we're warning you in advance, before you start assimilating the dope on this job—keep your eyes peeled for surprises—it's an entirely new airplane.

They Look Alike, but—

In general, the P-51H looks very much like the D, but there are specific differences which are easily distinguished. For one thing, the H has a lower drag airfoil section and a new wing plan form. The increased slope of the engine cowl centerline of the H—to improve visibility for the pilot—is quite apparent. And the improved fairing of the radiator ducts extending into the fuselage, and the larger size of the horizontal and vertical tail surfaces are features which definitely distinguish the new Mustang.

Structurally, the P-51H follows the new Army-Navy re-

This document contains information affecting the National Defense of the United States within the meaning of the Espionage Act, U.S.C. 50:31 and 32 as amended. Its transmission or the revelation of its contents in any manner to any unauthorized person is prohibited by law.

A copy of *Service News Weekly* near the end of the war carries the sage advice for employees to, "keep your eyes peeled . . . before you start assimilating the dope." The changeover to a whole new airplane design was, actually, quite a feat. Note that early H-model Mustang had tails the same size as P-51Ds. *Santa Maria Museum of Flight*

"In terms of jobs, this means that approximately fifty percent of all employees . . . will be laid off within the next few days. With few exceptions, the entire personnel of the Texas and Kansas plants will be laid off this week. Those exceptions include personnel transferred from Inglewood since our expansion of operations in 1940, and personnel necessary for inventory and closing out work."

Weeks before, the last P-51D had gone down the line at Inglewood nearly as quickly as the others, yet each employee

Above: Upupa Epops is the scientific name for the Hoopoe Bird. It's a very inside joke conceived by the airplane's pilot, Harrison "Bud" Tordoff. Before becoming an ace pilot during World War II, Tordoff was an ornithology (study of birds) student at Cornell University. That funny name stuck in his head. Better yet, *Upupa Epops* is a terrible creature by most accounts. The sly joke was that he'd named his beautiful and speedy fighter after a bird with puzzling flying characteristics, a cantankerous attitude, and a yucky antipredator secretion that smells like rotting meat. Of course, you had to have studied birds for years to get Tordoff's inside joke. *Heath Moffatt Photography/Flying Heritage Collection*

Opposite: Fuselage and wings meet at this conflux of critical airplane components. Here, the fuselage and wings of a P-51H Mustang join as one. In the foreground, racks of .50-calibers stand ready to be slipped into the wings of the new fighter airplane. *Santa Maria Museum of Flight*

took a moment or two longer to sign the aluminum skin of the airplane. By the time it reached the engine test stand, it was covered in the names of the people who had made this remarkable airplane a reality in such a short time.

Speed was the leitmotif for the Mustang. It took just two years to go from first flight to rolling out the five-hundredth airplane. By comparison, it took Lockheed four and three-quarters years to make the five-hundredth P-38 Lockheed and Republic two and a half years to makethe five-hundredth P-47 Thunderbolt. When the British told NAA that they had built "an airplane without a mistake," NAA officials joked that there wasn't any extra time to add any mistakes.

ESCORT
EXTRAORDINAIRE

IN THE YEARS BEFORE WORLD WAR II, American tacticians believed that well-armed heavy bomber airplanes could always push through to their bombing targets without any escort from friendly fighter airplanes. These men could not conceive that groups of big airplanes, flying in close formation and bristling with defensive guns, could ever be closely approached and significantly harmed by smaller interceptor airplanes.

Their theories were put to the test by the British soon after war erupted in Europe. On December 18, 1939, a group of twenty-four Vickers Wellington bombers set out to attack German warships at the northern seaport of Wilhelmshaven in broad daylight. Ruthlessly hammered by German fighters, only half of the RAF bombers made it home. By the end of 1939, RAF heavy bomber forces switched to finding their targets in the dark to avoid Germany's dreaded Luftwaffe, as daylight raids had proven too costly.

A great shot of *The Iowa Beaut* of the 355th Fighter Group. At the time, the airplane had been handed off from ace Lt. Col. Claiborne Kinnard to Lt. Robert Hulderman. The airplane was later adopted by a third pilot, who was hit by ground fire over Germany in late 1944. The P-51B spun in, killing Capt. Kevin Rafferty. *National Archives*

Mustangs Raise Hell in Heavens

Seven miles upstairs, Yank pilots ride the wings of fierce-charging Mustang fighters, dealing death to Nazis desperately trying to intercept our high-altitude heavy bombers. Here in the arctic cold of the stratosphere a chronicle of victory is sky-written by white vapor trails and by the searing flame of an enemy plane in its last earthbound plunge. The men and women of North American Aviation are proud of the "angels from hell" who pilot these avenging P-51 Mustangs—proud, too, of their own vital part on America's production front.

North American Aviation *Sets the Pace*

We make planes that make headlines...*The B-25 Mitchell bomber, the AT-6 Texan combat trainer, the P-51 Mustang fighter (A-36 fighter-bomber), and the B-24 Liberator bomber. North American Aviation, Inc. Member, Aircraft War Production Council, Inc.*

Above: *Peggy* of the 354th Fighter Group is fitted with seventy-five-gallon drop tanks soon after arrival in England. To avoid confusion with Bf 109 fighters, many of the newly arrived American airplanes had white noses, wing stripes, and tail stripes to avoid deadly confusion in the heat of battle.
National Archives

Inset: The "Mighty Eighth" was the greatest air armada of all time. Their missions came at a price. Half the casualties suffered by the USAAF in World War II were pilots of the Eighth Air Force. *Author's Collection*

Opposite: Merlin-powered Mustangs could now fight it out with the Germans from sea level to the stratosphere. This NAA ad highlights the ability of this "angel from hell" to follow the bombers to great heights. During World War II, Eighth Air Force bomber crews usually flew at twenty-five thousand to twenty-nine thousand feet. *Author's Collection*

The United States entered the war in Europe hoping it could succeed where the RAF had failed. The American VIII Bomber Command began daylight operations with Boeing B-17s in Europe in August of 1942, starting small and flying close to home. On August 17, twelve heavy bombers hit a railyard about thirty-five miles from the French coastline, the small force shepherded by RAF Spitfires. The mission was a success—only two airplanes were damaged, and none were lost.

Gradually, the US bomber forces grew and began to hit more heavily defended targets farther inland. For their success, they paid a steep price; more and more American airplanes were lost to German heavy antiaircraft fire and fighters as the missions grew. By January of 1943, it was clear that heavy bombers could not adequately defend themselves on their bombing runs. And friendly fighter escorts, who were hindered by weather and lack of fuel capacity, could not stay with the bombers continually to offer protection against the German airplanes rising to meet them.

Above: The grin makes me a little uneasy. The "threatening smile" of this P-51B Mustang flew with the 354th Fighter Group until well after D-Day. The airplane was eventually transferred to a recon unit when most of the other B and C models in the 354th had long since disappeared. *Santa Maria Museum of Flight*

Opposite: Lieutenant John Godfrey (left) and Capt. Don Gentile of the 4th Fighter Group made a lethal pair when they went hunting over Europe. Together they accounted for thirty-seven victories and were the most famous pair of pilots flying Mustangs during World War II. *National Archives*

Doubters wanted to follow the RAF into flying bombing missions under cover of darkness. But changes in tactics and fierce determination to succeed, despite many painful and costly defeats, allowed the Americans to continue their daytime attacks into the spring of 1943.

The arrival of the Republic P-47 Thunderbolt fighter, equipped with additional external fuel tanks, helped the bombers get through to their targets. Generally, the British Spitfire could work 175 miles from home; the Americans'

new fighter, lovingly called the "Jug" by pilots, could make it 375 miles with the use of external drop tanks. Bomber crews noted it was a great improvement, but after passing Frankfurt headed east, it was just them and the skilled and battle-hardened Luftwaffe left alone in the skies.

German pilots became skilled at "bouncing" escort flights early on, attacking them near the French coast. The attacks forced the escort fighters to drop their tanks and fight, thus reducing their range by some 140 miles. Others tended to

Above: The boys of the 354th Fighter Group talk over the latest developments in England between missions. The pilots, early in the war, mix their US Army garb with English flying kit to find the equipment that works best for them. *National Archives*

Right: How embarrassing. Top Mustang ace Don Gentile was showing off for the press after another successful mission when his low pass got a little too low. The propeller of his P-51B, named *Shangri-La*, dug into the sod. When crewmen reached the wreck, Gentile was leaning against what was left of his airplane. He told them, "I think I farbed up." *National Archives*

This image represents the whole reason for the Mustang's existence. The big Browning .50-calibers could protect a bomber formation or wreak havoc on ground targets. The inboard gun, added to P-51D airplanes, was built into the wing roughly one bullet length behind the others to allow for staggered storage of the airplane's ammunition. *Heath Moffatt Photography/Flying Heritage Collection*

wait until just outside range of American fighters. One line of a mission debrief report asked, "When and where did you encounter enemy fighters?" Often, the answer angrily scrawled by bomber pilots was, "Just after the Jugs left."

One year after American heavy bomber action started in Europe, 376 B-17 bombers attacked two targets deep into Germany. The mission for this daring double attack was to cripple airplane-production facilities in Regensburg and ball-bearing factories in Schweinfurt. After the escorting Spitfires and P-47s turned toward home, the exposed bomber formations were ravaged for hours by attacking German fighters. In this one afternoon, the Americans lost sixty bombers, more than double what had ever been lost before; more than 560 pilots were either killed or captured.

A second mission to Schweinfurt in October of 1943 yielded similar results. Some sixty bombers were shot down during the fierce battles with German defenders. Around seventeen more airplanes returned home so badly damaged that they would never fly again. More than 650 American airmen were lost, including approximately 590 killed in action. Airmen called the raid "Black Thursday."

The second raid to Schweinfurt shook the VIII Bomber Command to its core. Losses were so great that it would be nearly four months before US heavy bombers ventured deep into Germany again. When they returned, they would have to have proper escort on a near-constant basis. The timely arrival of combat-ready P-51 Mustang fighters would make this a possibility.

The first unit to use Merlin-powered Mustangs in large numbers was the 354th Fighter Group. On December 13, 1943, Lt. Glenn Eagleston scored the 354th's first probable victory when he repeatedly attacked a Messerschmitt Me 110 during a mission near Kiel. The enemy airplane was last observed in a flaming dive, sliding into the overcast.

Some of Eagleston's first experiences with the Mustang in combat exemplified a pair of the P-51's shortcomings in those early days. The reason he was not credited with the definite destruction of the German fighter he encountered was that during his fourth pass, his guns jammed. This problem was epidemic in the Mustang's first months of service, and considering that the airplane was only packing half the punch of a P-47 Thunderbolt to begin with, any gun stoppage was quite serious.

Indeed, the Mustang's four Browning .50-calibers tended to jam when pilots fired them in the middle of high-speed turns. The extra g-forces pulled on the airplane's belts of ammunition, causing the breech mechanism to block. The problem was solved by adding belt booster motors to the long feeds of ammunition as they left their storage boxes in the wings.

Eagleston was again at the forefront of the Mustang's combat quirks and oddities when, weeks after the Kiel encounter,

Before a mission to Germany, Col. Donald Blakeslee of the 4th Fighter Group prepares to close his canopy. The Ohio-born pilot had flown Spitfires with the RAF and was none too happy when the 4th received P-47s. He wanted Mustangs. Officials agreed, but would give them to the 4th only if they could be fully ready for combat just one day after the transition. Blakeslee famously told his men, "Learn to fly 'em on the way to the target." *National Archives*

his Mustang was bounced and blasted by an overanxious American P-47 pilot near Steinhuder Lake, Germany. Pilots on both sides admitted that the P-51, from many angles, looked a lot like a German Messerschmitt Bf 109; as an NAA publication put it, the Messerschmitt and Mustang looked similar "to an almost embarrassing extent."

In the heat of combat, the P-47 and Fw 190 were often confused as well. As a result, many of the first American fighters in England carried white bands on their noses, wings, and tails to separate the hunters from the hunted. The distinctive paint did not stop Eagleston's attacker, however. Limping home with smashed instruments and a serious oil leak, Eagleston managed to bail out of his severely damaged airplane over England and survive the case of mistaken identity.

As 1944 began, swarms of drop-tank-equipped Mustangs joined P-47s and some P-38s to shepherd American bombers on some of the most important missions of the war. With the use of 75-gallon external tanks, the Mustangs could make it to Kiel, Hamburg, Frankfurt, or Berlin. Soon, pressed-paper tanks, each holding 108 gallons, extended the coverage map even more. Pilots called the tanks their "babies." And when it came time for a pilot to drop his babies and fight, the P-51B Mustang was up to the task.

There would be plenty of chances to meet the Luftwaffe as bombing missions built back up in the first months of 1944. With the help of these far-flying Mustangs, the Allies embarked on an ambitious week of attacks in late February 1945—dubbed the Big Week—scattering more than ten thousand tons of bombs over targets in Germany and occupied Europe. The effort was two-pronged: while attacking German airplane production facilities, the Allies hoped to lure existing Luftwaffe combat airplanes into battle, leaving the German military with a shortage of frontline combat airplanes and experienced pilots.

As fighter escorts, Mustangs commonly cruised well above the big formations of bombers. The fast-moving P-51 squadrons were obliged to motor along in lazy zigzags in order to match the plodding pace of the B-17s and B-24s, snaking from side to side thousands of feet overhead. Unlike in the movies, Mustangs hardly ever got excessively close to the big bombers; that was a great way to get blasted by dozens of trigger-happy gunners. However, the grateful "bomber boys" could see their escorts high above, each with a single contrail snaking right and then meandering left over the hours of flight time and the miles below.

The high vantage point was a great place from which to spot any groups of German airplanes climbing up to intercept

The P-51 Mustang, fast becoming a symbol of the wartime United States, made numerous appearances on the covers of postwar comics aimed to appeal to young boys. Here, a P-51D dispatches a German Ju 88 bomber on the cover of a publication from the now-defunct Connecticut-based Charlton Comics Group. *Author's Collection*

the bombers. With a waggle of their wings, the Mustang pilots could shed their silver external tanks and begin a long dive toward the German fighters. By the time the two groups of airplanes met, the Mustangs would have quite an advantage, able to convert the potential energy of higher altitude into blistering speed. The beginnings of the clash were usually much more of a "slash and run" affair than the whirling dogfights seen in Hollywood movies. If things went well, the climbing Messerschmitt and Focke-Wulf fighters never even

Above: Ground crews of the 4th Fighter Group load a 108-gallon pressed-paper tank in place before a long mission into enemy territory. Once hung, the tank would be filled with fuel. Shops in Britain made thirteen thousand of the disposable tanks during World War II, allowing metals to be used for other wartime projects. *National Archives*

Right: Lieutenant Urban Drew of the 361st Fighter Group flies close to the camera in a P-51D usually assigned to Lt. Abe Rosenberger. Note the solid panel in the place of the usually perforated vent under the exhaust stacks—a modification made for cold-weather operations. The airplane was lost in August 1944 in a serious accident. *National Archives*

This famous shot shows Lt. William Grouseclose of the 4th Fighter Group, just a few months before he was shot down over Germany. His unit encountered more than thirty Bf 109s near Naumburg on September 11, 1944. He was later reported as a prisoner of war. *National Archives*

made it close to the bombers before the Germans' tight groupings were scattered all over the skies by the predatory P-51 pilots. Mustang pilots hunted in pairs: one pilot would be on the offensive while the second pilot covered the aggressor's tail. Nearby, the crewmen in the bombers watched intently as the "little friends" gave the Luftwaffe hell.

The arrival of these long-range Mustangs changed the face of strategic bombing in Europe. For German pilots, almost every encounter with American bombers now meant a potentially lethal confrontation with scores of capable and ferocious US Army pilots. The ranks of the Luftwaffe—planes, fuel, supplies, and pilots—were being threatened almost every day, both in the air and on the ground.

And the change in the balance of air power would soon have consequences on the war below. Diminishing the enemy's air

forces was critical to the success of opening up a new front in France in the summer of 1944. In those tenuous days when the Allies struggled to gain a foothold along the French coastline, they needed to have almost complete control of the air.

The campaign to eliminate the Luftwaffe in early 1944 was costly. During the Big Week, the Allies lost more than 380 bombers; however, the Germans sacrificed more than 350 fighters and lost nearly one hundred veteran pilots to seemingly ever-present Mustangs. The key to the ambitious attacks was that, in the months that followed, the Allies could bring many more airplanes and pilots into the fight. The Luftwaffe, however, was severely diminished.

The sheer volume of American airplanes arriving in England allowed for a change in tactics at around the same time as the Big Week. Previously, escort airplanes had been

Above: Pilots can't help but talk with their hands when talking about flying. Here, Flight Officer Glenn Stapp (left) and Lt. William Manahan of the 353rd Fighter Group talk shop in front of the weather-worn P-51D *Lady Gwen II*. *National Archives*

Left: Lieutenant James Fisk in Italy clowns for the cameras after his Mustang was sieved by ground fire during a mission to attack German ground forces. As many have said, combat flying is a young man's game. By the time you are an old man of twenty-six years or more, you have the common sense to know that next time, you might not be so lucky. *National Archives*

ATTENTION LUFTWAFFE! Keep away from this plane. Expect to see it on the farthest trip American bombers make. Expect to see it up high—40,000 feet—but don't expect to see it for long, because the Mustang travels at over 425 m. p. h.

And you can expect to see more and more Mustangs, too. The men and women at North American are stepping up production every month. So when you see this high fighting, far flying Mustang, look out, Luftwaffe. Get out of there quick!

North American P-51 Mustang Fighter

ATTENTION AMERICANS! BONDS bought these planes. WASTE FATS helped arm them. WASTE PAPER helped ship them. GASOLINE flies them. Will YOU help to deliver the next squadron?

FULL-VISION "TEAR-DROP" COCKPIT ENCLOSURE   DROPABLE WING GAS TANKS, FOR INCREASED RANGE   SIX .50 CALIBER MACHINE GUNS

North American Aviation *Sets the Pace*

WE MAKE PLANES THAT MAKE HEADLINES . . . *the B-25 Mitchell bomber, AT-6 Texan combat trainer, P-51 Mustang fighter (A-36 fighter-bomber), and the B-24 Liberator bomber. North American Aviation, Inc. Member, Aircraft War Production Council, Inc.*

Above: Captain Jack "Wild Bill" Crump flies *Jackie*, a P-51D of the 356th Fighter Group. The airplane has a painting of a howling coyote under the cockpit. Crump adopted a coyote pup while he was in training in Nebraska. The pup, named Jeep, was smuggled aboard the *Queen Elizabeth* and, amazingly, flew a handful of combat missions in the cockpit of Crump's Mustang. *Flying Heritage Collection*

Opposite: Putting the Luftwaffe on notice. Americans, rationing fats, waste paper, and gasoline, viewed this ad featuring a mock bulletin to German pilots, touting the speed and prowess of the Mustang fighter as manufacturing efforts ramped up stateside. *Author's Collection*

ordered to stick with their assigned bomber formations at any cost. Enemy pilots sniffing around bomber formations—but never directly attacking—were frustratingly just out of reach for restless escort pilots. Now, however, there were enough capable fighters, including growing squadrons of Mustangs, to take on enemy airplanes on almost any occasion. The escorts could care for the bombers adequately while also being able to chase every time Luftwaffe fighters showed themselves, and commanders told their pilots to find German airplanes and destroy them, anywhere, at any time, in the air or on the ground.

This free-for-all was just what the P-51 pilots liked; they could go hunting. Soon, Mustangs were a common sight, not only at thirty thousand feet but right down on the deck, blasting trains, machine-gunning flak batteries, and slinking around enemy airfields like a pack of hungry wolves. Unfortunately, operating so close to the ground magnified one of the Mustang's worst weaknesses. Everyone, it seemed, got to take a pot shot at a fighter once it was only a few hundred feet from the deck, and one bullet through the airplane's radiator or even a single tiny shrapnel nick in a coolant line would start a process that nearly always led to disaster. As coolant dribbled into the slipstream, engine and oil temperatures spiked—soon enough, the Merlin would eat itself alive. When the propeller stopped cold, pilots called it the "Big X." And when an American pilot bailed out

Above: Captain James Duffy Jr. of the 355th Fighter Group is photographed here with his P-51D and his pet bulldog, Yank. Pilots of the unit acquired the well-bred English canine at a Duxford dog show. Yank was supposedly the offspring of one of Winston Churchill's dogs. The 354th Fighter Squadron quickly adopted the nickname The Bulldogs. Eventually, Yank was smuggled back to the United States in a duffel bag. *National Archives*

Opposite: The airplanes of the 4th Fighter Group, at their base in Debden, England, made the cover of NAA's *Skyline* in early 1945. The crew's guns and ammo are laid out on pierced steel planking, put down to combat muddy terrain around the airfield. *Santa Maria Museum of Flight*

on the wrong side of the English Channel, there was very little chance he'd return to fly again.

One Mustang pilot was saved from becoming a prisoner of war from the sheer tenacity of his squadron mates. Captain Bert Marshall Jr.'s airplane was racked by gunfire during a low-level attack on a train yard north of Paris. "It was like somebody tossed a handful of gravel hard against the plane," he later told reporters. As he was struggling to set the Mustang down, one of his men told him over the radio, "Land on a road, coach. I'll land an' pick you up." Marshall dismissed him, but the pilot, Lt. Royce Priest, wouldn't take no for an answer. As soon as the captain's Mustang slid to a stop, Priest asked, "How's the dirt down there? Too soft to land?" Once again, Marshall told him to go home.

However, as he watched unbelievingly, Priest chose a nearby field and brought his Mustang, nicknamed *Eaglebeak*, in for a landing on the grass. Marshall made a run for the airplane, still with no intention of getting in. "I remembered I only had two American cigarettes, and I didn't like the idea of sticking around France with only two American cigarettes."

When Marshall finally reached Priest, the young pilot was using *Eaglebeak*'s engine and prop to blast rocks and dirt at a group of French farmers who were getting a little too close for his liking. Marshall climbed onto the wing of Priest's Mustang, and they debated their situation. "There was a reasonable amount of profanity involved," Priest later recounted later. After much coaxing, Priest convinced Marshall to let him toss out his parachute so the captain could climb in. Then, Priest

NORTH AMERICAN *Skyline*

JANUARY
FEBRUARY
1945

Left: Some World War II ads used the power and mystique of Mustang pilots tasked to eliminate the Luftwaffe to sell manly products. This Father's Day advertisement is "for men who are going places." *Author's Collection*

Opposite: Sky Bouncer, made famous in the iconic "Bottisham Four" Mustang formation photo, was flown by the 361st Fighter Group, 375th Fighter Squadron operations officer Capt. Bruce "Red" Rowlett. There was perhaps no more fitting name for the P-51 Mustang and its job over Europe. *Sky Bouncer* was wrecked on takeoff on April 3, 1945. *National Archives*

Below: In the warbird community, invasion stripes are applied in nice, straight, nearly perfect lines. Not so in the field. The paint was quickly and sloppily applied the night before D-Day. This image, set up for the press days later, shows one crewman who isn't doing all that bad a job, considering his work load. *National Archives*

sat in Marshall's lap. The pair of pilots managed to reach all the important cockpit controls in order to take off. When they gunned the engine, the canopy slid back and bashed Priest in the head. Marshall managed to hold the canopy while Priest took off and headed for friendly territory.

The pair, in the single-seat Mustang, managed to fly to England and reach their home field. When Priest couldn't reach the flap handle, Marshall managed to take care of it. As they parked, they were sure a sight for Priest's ground crew. The men couldn't quite believe it.

For Priest's strange rescue of a fellow Mustang pilot, Gen. Jimmy Doolittle awarded him the Distinguished Service Cross. Priest later related that during the ceremony, Doolittle said to him, "I never thought I would have to issue an order that said, 'Don't land behind enemy lines to attempt a rescue.'" Smiling, Doolittle added, "Who would be that stupid?"

Above: A cold stare from the pilot who flies *Atlanta Peach,* a P-51B assigned to the 354th Fighter Group. In twenty-seven bombing missions and fighter sweeps, Lt. William King has dispatched a locomotive, two troop carriers, one and a half German warplanes, and at least five enemy soldiers. *National Archives*

Left: This airplane flew with the 356th Fighter Group, 359th Fighter Squadron. The interesting part of this image is that the airplane has the wrong prop for its serial number. The P-51K came from the Dallas factory with an unpopular Aeroproducts propeller. After an accident at RAF Martlesham Heath in December 1944, the badly damaged airplane was rebuilt and equipped with a Hamilton Standard prop. *Flying Heritage Collection*

Right: This rare image taken from a Mustang's wing-mounted gun camera shows not only a German Me 262 jet fighter but also another P-51 being stalked by the Nazi airplane. This, insisted squadron commanders, is why you always fly in pairs. The victim, German pilot Lt. Joachim Fingerlos, was shot down by Mustang pilot Lt. C. W. Mueller of the 353rd Fighter Group. *National Archives*

Right: Today, a Mustang painted in the scheme of the 353rd Fighter Group's *Willit Run?* resides in the National Air and Space Museum's World War II Aviation Gallery. This is an image of the real airplane it represents in service during the war. The yellow and black checkers used on the noses of 353rd airplanes were considered too difficult to see from great distances. As a result, ground crewmen were ordered to add more color to the fighters, obliterating some of the nose art on the Mustangs in the unit. *National Archives*

Despite the dangers of low-level missions, the attempts to eradicate German aviation assets were almost a complete success. Each month, Mustangs (along with P-47s, P-38s, and Spitfires) dispatched a sizable chunk of the Luftwaffe's airplanes and experienced pilots. The loss of so many pilots, in particular, was devastating to Germany's war effort. New pilots were green, with just a handful of flying hours in training before they were thrust into the buzz saw of combat.

On June 6, 1944, when Allied soldiers stormed ashore at Normandy on D-Day, the Luftwaffe was only able to muster around one hundred sorties to try to stop them. They were met by 171 *squadrons* of British and US Army fighter airplanes protecting the ships, patrolling the beach, and ranging inland to slow enemy ground units moving up to reinforce the Germans at the beachhead.

As the Allies struggled to expand their foothold in France, many fighter groups based in England replaced their B- and

Above: Old Red Nose, a P-51D built in the last days of World War II, is an icon to any warbird enthusiast. After years in the Royal Canadian Air Force, Texan Lloyd Nolan and some friends bought the airplane for $2,500 in 1957. After a few weeks, someone painted "Confederate Air Force" on the tail. The name stuck. *Old Red Nose* was the one warbird that started it all. *EAA/Jim Koepnick Photo*

Inset: While the Eighth Air Force seems to get all the credit for the air war over Europe, there was a whole other corps of bomber and fighter pilots hitting Germany from below. *Author's Collection*

A flight of 31st Fighter Group Mustangs, loaded with fuel, go out looking for trouble. The month before, in July 1944, the group had destroyed eighty-two German airplanes. In August, they flew escort for three bombing missions to the Ploesti oil fields in Romania. *National Archives*

Crewmen dig in to the accessory section of a P-51D's Merlin at a base in England. The airplane has a 108-gallon pressed-paper drop tank installed. Made in Britain, these tanks were good for one flight. Pilots were instructed to never land with them—they might not be able to take the stress. *Flying Heritage Collection*

C-model Mustangs with new D models. The improved version of the NAA fighter had the bubble canopy and more firepower—six Browning .50-caliber guns in the place of the four carried by the older P-51s. While P-51D airplanes became the norm, a few B- and C-model "survivors" continued service in fighter units until the end of the war.

Some of the older Mustangs were shuffled to Ninth Air Force units, charged with supporting advancing armies in France and Germany. The task of dueling with German tanks, trains, and trucks was more suited to hearty P-47 Thunderbolts, but some squadrons insisted on Mustangs. Additionally, the speedy P-51 was the preferred fighter for the Ninth's tactical reconnaissance units, barreling through at low level to shoot photos of newly bombed bridges and train yards.

For England-based Eighth Air Force fighter units, as well, the Mustang became king. Tasked with continuing to shepherd ever-growing formations of American bombers into Germany, the P-51D was the weapon of choice to fly incredible distances and could more than hold its own with anything that came up to challenge it. By the end of the war, every fighter unit in the Eighth Air Force with the exception of one flew Mustangs.

By 1945, true "thousand-plane raids" featured as many as fourteen Mustang units, each sporting a cavalcade of colors swathed over their bare metal skins. The paint was meant to help tell one group of pilots from the next in the busy skies near the target. The noses of 359th Fighter Group airplanes were green, while the 4th Fighter Group took red, the 361st yellow, the 355th white, and the 352nd blue. Checkers identified the 78th Fighter Group (black and white), 356th (red and blue), 353rd (yellow and black), 55th (green and yellow), 339th (white and red), and 357th (red and yellow). Rounding out the kaleidoscope were the black stripes of the 20th Fighter Group

A pair of warbirds, flown by the Flying Heritage Collection, set up for a photo session near Seattle. Today, Republic P-47s are rarer than Mustangs because they were considered obsolete soon after World War II came to an end. The big Thunderbolts were scrapped in large numbers during the 1950s. *Jim Larsen/Flying Heritage Collection*

and the white and blue of the 364th Fighter Group. Perhaps because there seemed to be no other color combinations left, the 479th Fighter Group Mustangs were almost bare, with just a single color on the tail rudder (black, red, or yellow, depending on the squadron).

With new vigor and confidence, huge formations of American bombers would thunder wherever they pleased, disgorging tons of high explosives. If any threats dared come up to meet them, scores of Mustangs would pounce, jockeying for a position to get a shot. Many young P-51 pilots, new to combat, never even saw any Luftwaffe airplanes in the air; they were mostly gone. A few Mustang pilots, though, had strange encounters with Germany's high-tech wonders.

Captain William Anderson spotted something unusual while he and fellow pilots were patrolling over the English countryside. "Excuse me for a moment, gentlemen," he said over the radio. Anderson rolled his Mustang out of formation to follow what he had seen—a strange, pilotless, propeller-less airplane—as it streaked under them. His gunfire made the intruder explode violently. Days later, the press claimed that the Mustang pilot was the first Allied pilot to catch and destroy a V-1 flying bomb. The date of the encounter was June 17, 1944.

Other odd encounters with high-tech German airplanes followed. Messerschmitt Me 262s, sleek sharks of the sky, were more than one hundred miles per hour faster than Mustangs and carried four hard-hitting 30mm guns. As they went for the American bombers, escort pilots often struggled to keep up.

It was too little too late, though. While jet-powered German fighters could outclass older, piston-powered models used by the Allies, the jets would never have the upper hand in numbers. By the end of the conflict, Luftwaffe fighters were commonly outnumbered by thirty or more to one. Shortages of fuel and supplies and the lack of safe operating areas limited the ability of jet airplanes to change the outlook of the air war. Perhaps even more importantly, Germany lacked experienced combat pilots to fly these "superplanes," their ranks ground down to nothing through years of tough combat.

Allied pilots were quick to exploit the weaknesses of jets, too. At combat speeds, a Mustang was no match for an Me 262, but if a P-51 pilot could dive, follow, and push his airplane to the limit, the fuel-gobbling jet would soon run out of gas and room to maneuver. Quite often, marauding Mustangs would tail jets back to base, using their range and speed to keep the jets in sight, and then buzz-saw into the defenseless German airplanes as they circled their airfield with their landing gear down.

As 4th Fighter Group pilot Maj. Fred Glover told the press about his encounter with a rocket-powered Me 163: "I kept in sight of him and when he turned off his jet power unit [*sic*], I caught up, slipped behind him, and blew him to hell." The

Beyond the carcass of a burned-out Focke-Wulf Fw 190, a P-51D of the 356th Fighter Group gets serviced on German soil near the end of the war. Airfield Y-74 was near Frankfurt, Germany. *National Archives*

TUSKEGEE AIRMEN

Opposite: Tuskegee Airmen Capt. Andrew Turner and Lt. Clarence "Lucky" Lester of the 332nd Fighter Group discuss tactics near P-51C *Skipper's Darlin' III* in Italy in 1944. At the time, Lester had shot down three German airplanes in air-to-air combat. *National Archives*

The Allies worked to attack Germany from nearly every side. The Russians pushed back in the east, British and American bombers (and their fighter escorts) struck from the west, and in the south, Italy surrendered as Allied armies stormed ashore in September of 1943. Quickly pushing northward, the Americans cleared room for bomber bases, allowing airplanes to strike upward into Europe's underbelly. Like their counterparts in England, squadrons of Mustangs moved into southern Italy to shepherd the B-17s and B-24s on their flights to fuel-production facilities, airplane factories, and military sites that were previously out of range from the west.

Of the many units to operate the Mustang in the Mediterranean theater of operations, one was unique. Some of the pilots of the 332nd Fighter Group were veterans of combat in the Mediterranean, Sicily, and Italy, but even the newest pilots in the unit were no stranger to fighting for their rightful place in the USAAF. What made the 332nd different, however, was that it was made up entirely of African American pilots and support personnel trained near Tuskegee, Alabama. Parts of the unit had flown P-40s, P-39s, and P-47s before transitioning to Mustangs in the summer of 1944. The pilots painted their P-51s with distinctive red spinners and tail surfaces before joining other fighter units escorting heavy bombers over enemy territory.

The Tuskegee Airmen excelled at the task of shielding the bombers from scores of attacking fighter airplanes over Italy and beyond. For many years the press claimed the unit had never lost a bomber under their care to enemy airplanes. While it was later found that a handful of American bombers were lost during their escort missions, the record of the 332nd is second to none. More than 97.5 percent of the airplanes shepherded by the unit called the "Red Tails" survived German fighter attacks over tough targets such as Munich, Vienna, and Berlin.

The Berlin mission took place on March 24, 1945. The heavily defended Daimler-Benz tank factory near the German capitol was the target of nearly 150 Fifteenth Air Force bombers and their escort that day, and among the formations that flew were 54 Mustangs of the 332nd. Near the target, Red Tail pilots later reported sighting a mass of Me 262 jet fighters, a handful of Fw 190s, a Me 163 rocket plane, and, strangely, a single P-51 Mustang painted black with German markings.

The Tuskegee pilots took on many of the jet-powered Messerschmitts as they moved in to attack the bombers. Though slower by more than one hundred miles per hour, several 332nd pilots positioned their Mustangs to fight it out with Germany's superplanes. In the mission narrative, the unit claimed destruction of three Me 262s, with five more damaged or possibly destroyed. The Red Tails reported no losses among their own airplanes.

For their participation in "one of the longest bombing missions of the Fifteenth Air Force," as well as successful combats versus much more advanced German attackers, the pilots of the 332nd were awarded the Distinguished Unit Citation. At the end of fighting, according to the USAAF, the Tuskegee Airmen had shot down 112 enemy airplanes and destroyed 150 more on the ground. Some 150 pilots were killed in combat or accidents, while 32 more became prisoners of war.

Above: Lieutenant William Whitaker poses with his 356th Fighter Group Mustang sometime in 1945. The 356th airplanes carried distinctive blue checkers on a red background. The squadrons within the group flew with different-colored prop spinners, rudders, and canopy rails. Yellow was the color worn on 359th Fighter Squadron airplanes. *Flying Heritage Collection*

Opposite: Mustangs of the 31st Fighter Group roll away from the camera in pairs of two, leader and wingman. Four P-51s was a flight, and a typical squadron had sixteen airplanes. Later in the war, some fighter squadrons fielded twenty-five Mustangs at a time. *National Archives*

Mustang pilots of the 4th went so far as to make this type of attack an out-and-out practiced routine. They rehearsed attacks on jet bases using their own airfield in England as the training ground—coming in at over four hundred miles per hour and just a few feet over the trees. All the while, another group of P-51s rode shotgun, picking out targets and taking care of any big guns on the ground.

When the 4th Fighter Group Mustangs hit Leipheim airfield in Germany, the only thing that didn't go according to the well-oiled plan was the fact that the smoke from so many burning German jets ruined the fighter pilots' ability to see more targets. Along with additional P-51s from the 355th Fighter Group, they spent forty-five minutes beating up the airfield. Some forty Me 262s were destroyed, including one jet shot from the skies by the overhead contingent when the unlucky German pilot stumbled into the slaughter.

Mustang pilots are credited with more than 130 kills of German jets, including 118.5 Messerschmitt Me 262s, 12 Arado Ar 234s, and 5 Messerschmitt Me 163 rocket fighters. Eight Mustang pilots shot down more than one Nazi jet. By contrast, P-47 Thunderbolt pilots downed a combined 20.5 jets in Europe. No P-38 pilot had a confirmed kill on a jet airplane.

As the war in Europe reached its final months and Allied armies approached Berlin from east and west, American bombers continued to pound German cities and factories almost every day. On April 7, 1945, Germany sent 120 student pilots aloft to face more than a thousand American airplanes. Most of the German novice pilots didn't come home. Three days later, half the jets sent to defend Berlin were ravaged by Mustangs.

Nearly two weeks after that, the last five American bombers to fall to Luftwaffe opposition were downed during a raid over Czechoslovakia. The attack on the Skoda tank factory on April 25, 1945, was the last full-scale bombing mission taken on by the Americans in Europe. Soon after, the war in Europe was over.

When the fighting ceased and US intelligence officers questioned former Luftwaffe chief Hermann Göring, they asked him when he knew the war was lost. Göring replied, "When I saw your bombers over Berlin protected by your long-range fighters [Mustangs], I knew then that the Luftwaffe would be unable to stop your bombers. Our weapons plants would be destroyed; our defeat was inevitable."

5

SWEEPING
THE SKIES

ON THE OTHER SIDE OF THE WORLD, US Army Air Forces units needed the Mustang, too. Just as the far-flying fighter put targets such as Schweinfurt and Berlin within reach in Europe, the Mustang could also shrink mile after mile of the nearly boundless Pacific Ocean and bypass vast expanses of rugged and hostile terrain in East Asia.

As in North Africa, the first Mustangs to reach China were Allison-powered A-36s and P-51As, entering combat in the summer of 1943. With much of China's coast and all its major ports under the thumb of brutal Japanese occupation, the new airplanes were shipped to India and then flown to the war zone over some of the most unforgiving terrain in the world.

Most of the Allied military actions on the ground in the China-Burma-India theater of operations (CBI) were undertaken by Nationalist Chinese armies. Though not as technologically advanced as Japan or many western nations,

A color shot of David "Tex" Hill's well-worn P-51B in China. The imposing shark-mouth motif, used by both P-40 and later P-51 units in China, was inspired by RAF units in North Africa at the beginning of the war. *National Archives*

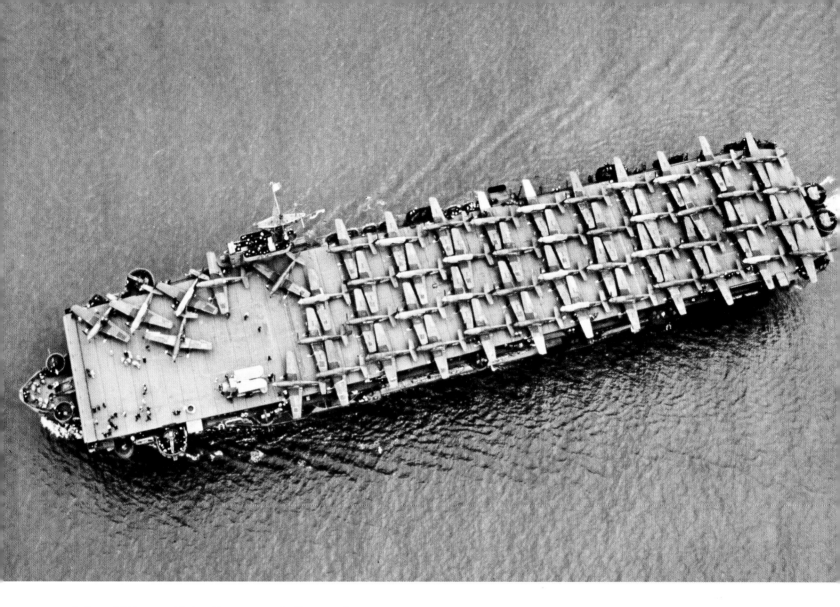

Early-model Mustangs hitch a ride across the Pacific on the flight deck of the escort carrier USS *Altamaha*. The vessel passed under the Golden Gate Bridge in July 1943 bound for Australia and then India. These airplanes were the first P-51s to make it to the CBI. *National Archives*

China could recruit a nearly endless supply of young men to tackle the dirty work of fighting the Japanese in their homeland. However, China's shortcomings in the field of aviation were significant—they possessed almost nothing to counter modern Japanese fighter and bomber airplanes. Dating back to the days of the American Volunteer Group (Flying Tigers) in 1941 and 1942, China had required aerial assistance in the form of contemporary Allied airplanes to protect its armies below and take on the Japanese in the air. Thus, Mustangs reinforced squadrons of weather-beaten Curtiss P-40s working to stall enemy advances in the CBI.

Commonly, Mustangs and Apaches were used for low-level work, sometimes escorting bombers but often working independently, hitting bridges, airfields, and troop concentrations. Like nearly every American airplane thrown into the fray before them, early Allison-powered Mustangs were no match for Japan's top-of-the-line naval fighter, the A6M "Zero." In the midst of lugging bombs or strafing ground targets, early Mustang pilots were sometimes forced to revert to survival mode when the light and nimble Mitsubishi fighters appeared on the scene. One of the first squadrons to employ Mustangs in China was temporarily knocked out of commission in late 1943 due to the losses suffered from a number of run-ins with this dangerous foe. Things changed dramatically when Merlin-powered Mustangs arrived in early 1944—the new airplanes had enough speed and power to take on Japan's best fighters.

In the past, enemy pilots operating in China had been known to try to lure US airmen into a jam using a baiting tactic. The Americans would notice an enemy airplane cruising alone at low altitude; as they moved to pick off this tempting target, a mass of Japanese fighters would jump them

from above. However, P-51 pilots operating Merlin-powered Mustangs learned that they could dive at the decoy, tear it to pieces, and then power away at high speed before their attackers from above ever had the chance to spring their trap. Speed and power—this doctrine had been uttered over and over again by American pilots in China from the days of the Flying Tigers. The use of firepower and horsepower could counter the advantages of the nimble and light Japanese fighters.

Pilots were instructed to fly fast and not turn back until they had plenty of room to do so. In fact, Army leaders continuously preached to Mustang pilots to never get under 350 miles per hour in aerial combat. And never get into a turning duel with a Zero or other nimble Japanese fighters.

It seemed that the Americans had finally found the solution to counteract the domination of the Zero in China. The constant difficulty there was getting enough Mustangs to effectively get the job done. The vast majority of the P-51s built in the United States were needed in the European theater to help with the

Above: Airfields in China were most often built completely by hand. Here, Miao workers flatten Laohwangping airfield with a ten-ton roller. The runway in south-central China was used by fighters, including the Mustangs of the 23rd Fighter Group. *National Archives*

Inset: True to its Flying Tiger heritage, the US Army's Fourteenth Air Force patch featured a winged tiger, claws extended. The pilots of the Fourteenth worked over some of the roughest terrain in the world while flying in the CBI. *Author's Collection*

Above: Tex Hill, commander of the 23rd Fighter Group, poses with his shark-mouthed P-51B Mustang. At the time, in the summer 1944, it was one of the very few Merlin-powered Mustangs in China. Hill joined the Flying Tigers before the United States entered the war and later served with the USAAF in China. He is credited with downing eighteen and three-quarters Japanese airplanes. *National Archives*

Previous pages: Mrs. Virginia, a P-51A Mustang, cruises near Chin Hills in China. The airplane was flown by Maj. Bob Petit, the operations officer of the fighter section of the 1st Air Commando Group. The airplanes carry a pair of seventy-five-gallon external tanks. *National Archives*

Opposite: Three-shot rocket launchers, one on each wing, could make the Mustang a "Flying Bazooka." While they didn't have as much punching power as five-inch HVAR rockets, the long tubes made the smaller missiles a bit more accurate. An intriguing unintentional sidelight to this ad is the mention of the P-51 carrying thousand-pound bombs, though the airplane's pylons were "not recommended" for the big bombs or for 110-gallon external tanks. *Author's Collection*

bombing effort against the Nazis in Europe, and pilots and military leaders in the CBI always felt they were secondary to their colleagues who flew missions over Fortress Europe.

Thousands of Mustangs were delivered to bases in England, while in the CBI at the end of 1944, there were only approximately 250. Worse yet, transport of spare parts for the airplanes was difficult; every gallon of gas, part, and bullet had to find its way to the front through a difficult and dangerous supply line over the Himalayas before entering combat. That said, the small handful of P-51s that did make it through were critical to the war effort. Like the strategies employed in Europe, the fighting Mustangs in the CBI cleared the skies of threats in less than two years and robbed the Japanese of some of its most capable pilots.

By the first months of 1945, it was a rare occurrence to encounter a Japanese airplane over China. And, as war in

Flying Bazooka

MYITKYINA, BURMA...a Jap garrison is almost surrounded by Chinese and American forces, but Jap supplies are still coming through. A P-51 Mustang squadron is out to break the supply line. Bazooka tubes are mounted on the Mustangs' wings and the Yanks are out shooting sky rockets at the Nips. Water-borne supplies get holes punched in them. Trucks and trains are blasted out of this world. A new incurable headache for the Japs is born...flying bazookas.

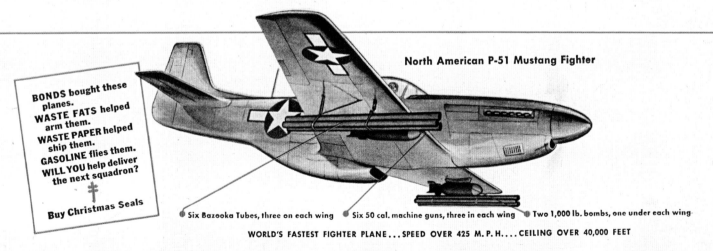

North American P-51 Mustang Fighter

BONDS bought these planes.
WASTE FATS helped arm them.
WASTE PAPER helped ship them.
GASOLINE flies them.
WILL YOU help deliver the next squadron?

Buy Christmas Seals

• Six Bazooka Tubes, three on each wing • Six 50 cal. machine guns, three in each wing • Two 1,000 lb. bombs, one under each wing

WORLD'S FASTEST FIGHTER PLANE...SPEED OVER 425 M.P.H....CEILING OVER 40,000 FEET

North American Aviation *Sets the Pace*

<u>PLANES THAT MAKE HEADLINES</u>...*the P-51 Mustang fighter (A-36 fighter-bomber), B-25 and PBJ Mitchell bomber, the AT-6 and SNJ Texan combat trainer. North American Aviation, Inc. Member, Aircraft War Production Council, Inc.*

NORTH AMERICAN *Skyline*

MAY
JUNE
1945

TWO CHINA FIGHTERS

Europe seemed to be coming to an end, military officials diverted more and more critically needed Mustangs to Asia—as many as five hundred per month in the last half year of the conflict. As air threats diminished and P-51s became more plentiful, CBI pilots concocted a series of raids to exhibit the far-ranging abilities of the Mustang. On December 19, 1944, some forty bomb-laden P-51s attacked the port of Hong Kong; according to wartime reports (which, admittedly, were often exaggerated), the Mustangs sank a Japanese destroyer and two freighters.

Carrying drop tanks in the place of bombs, forty Air Commando Mustangs flew from Cox's Bazaar (near the India-Burma border) to the airfield at Don Muang, near Bangkok, Thailand. The raid was the longest offensive fighter mission of the war to that point, spanning more than 1,500 miles. The successful attack eliminated half of the remaining service-able Japanese airplanes in the Thailand-Burma area.

As Japanese resistance weakened, enterprising airmen and ground crewmen of the Fourteenth Air Force impro-vised additional hard points on their Mustangs to keep them in the fight. The modified airplanes could carry two 250-pound bombs and two groups of twelve 20-pound AN-M1A1 antipersonnel cluster bombs. Alternately, the air-planes could heft the two 250-pound bombs along with two seventy-five-gallon external fuel tanks. Or, most impress-ively, the Mustangs could fly with four seventy-five-gallon tanks, giving them the total fuel capacity to stay aloft for more than eight hours and over 2,500 miles.

While USAAF units in the CBI complained about the slow supply of P-51s, the top brass could spare absolutely no Mustangs for the units in the Pacific until the last days of 1944. Army fighting forces among the islands in the Southwest Pacific were forced to make do with outdated types that often put them at a dangerous disadvantage when paired against nimble and long-ranged Japanese fighters.

The first pilots to use Mustangs in combat in the Pacific were part of a mixed unit, the 3rd Air Commando Group, in the Philippines. Their fighters, operating along with scout and cargo airplanes, moved to Leyte as the enemy was for-cibly pushed out by the US Sixth Army. With the Japanese war effort waning in the last year of the war, the 3rd found it diffi-cult to keep its foe within range, and encounters with enemy airplanes were very rare. Mustang pilots in the 3rd saw just twelve airplanes in the air and managed to catch and destroy seven of them. Their airplanes were used almost exclusively on ground-attack missions, dropping over two thousand tons

Above: Major General Claire Chennault and Brig. Gen. Edgar Glenn talk with mechanics and inspect engine repairs on a P-51B Mustang of the 23rd Fighter Group. The visit took place at an airfield near Kunming, China, on November 3, 1944. After the Flying Tigers disbanded, Chennault continued to be an advocate for the use of air power in China and often butted heads with American leaders in the region. *National Archives*

Opposite: On the cover of NAA's *Skyline* magazine, a Chinese infantryman stands before "foreign technology," illustrating a stark contrast been old ideas and the new warfare. The strength of Chiang Kai-shek's numbers were not enough to extract Japan from strategic locations, and this need for superior weaponry created a dependence on airplanes from the West. After the defeat of Germany, the role of most manufacturing refocused on combat with Japan in the CBI and Pacific. *Santa Maria Museum of Flight*

Following pages: My Ned, a P-51D of the 311th Fighter Group, cruises over China in 1945. Note the airplane's direction-finding ADF loop antenna forward of the vertical stabilizer, commonly seen on many fighters serving in the CBI. *National Archives*

of bombs on targets in Formosa and Luzon as well as attack-ing enemy shipping.

One Mustang pilot in the Philippines had much better luck. On January 11, 1945, Maj. William Shomo and his wingman took off in their reconnaissance-equipped F-6D Mustangs, headed for a Japanese-held airfield in northern Luzon. The pair encountered a single Japanese bomber being escorted by twelve fighters. Though greatly outnumbered, Shomo and his partner approached the formation from below. Hammering

MIXED BAG

Below: This little model was released by The Lindberg Line of Skokie, Illinois. Paul Lindberg started out making balsa kits but moved into plastic injection molding after the war. With just twenty-four pieces, this kit made a reasonable facsimile of the Mustang, complete with three-shot bazookas and a small selection of decals. *Author's Collection*

Lower right: Major James Howard was dubbed the "One Man Air Force" for his exploits over Europe. His Mustang, a P-51B named *Ding Hao!*, flew with a collection of victory markings signifying the destruction of both German and Japanese airplanes. "Ding hao" was an American slang term taken from the Chinese phrase *ting hao de*, meaning "very good." *National Archives*

A few Mustang pilots had the distinction of flying and fighting in more than one theater during the war. As a result, at the end of the conflict, a handful of P-51s wore a strange mix of German and Japanese kill markings under their cockpits.

Pilot James Howard was born in Canton, China, to missionary parents in 1913. Flying with the US Navy before Pearl Harbor, Howard resigned his commission and served with Claire Chennault's American Volunteer Group, the Flying Tigers, in China. Flying the P-40, he completed fifty-six combat missions. The number of Japanese airplanes that fell to this "skinny, young kid" varies widely by source. Not only did Howard shoot down Japanese airplanes in air-to-air combat, he is also credited with destroying a number of Japanese airplanes on the ground.

In 1943, Howard joined the USAAF and served in the 354th Fighter Group, flying Mustangs from England. He is perhaps most famous for an event during which he single-handedly took on thirty German fighters to protect a formation of B-17 bombers near Halberstadt, Germany. Separated from his companions, as he put it, "I got lost and I got busy." As the bomber crews looked on, Howard's P-51B, named *Ding Hao*, took on waves of Me 110s, Fw 190s, and Bf 109s. Howard headed off attacks until his ammunition was gone and then stayed longer, bluffing the Germans into breaking off their firing runs. The engagement was made famous by a cover story in *True Magazine* entitled "One-Man Air Force." For his bravery, Howard became the first Mustang pilot to receive the Medal of Honor.

He later told a reporter, "The Germans are good fighters. You really have to riddle them to bring 'em down, whereas a few hits on a Jap plane will finish it. The Japs aren't very good shots either, but they are more alert than the German pilots. The Japs flew different planes and the formations were different, so it is hard to compare the fight here with the fighting in the air out in the Pacific."

Howard wasn't the only pilot to pull double duty. Perhaps the most famous Mustang livery in World War II was *Big Beautiful Doll*, flown by John D. Landers. The side of this P-51 displayed a massive field of victory markings, a mix of German and Japanese. Landers's first victories came in the Pacific, where he flew P-40s. Later, he piloted a P-38 in Europe. His first kill in a Mustang, his eleventh overall, came in the fall of 1944. Amazingly, Landers was headed

AN AUTHENTIC CONSTRUCTION PLASTIC AIRPLANE KIT

north american
P-51D MUSTANG

FOR BEST RESULTS USE LINDBERG'S PLASTIC CEMENT

BY PAUL LINDBERG

the LINDBERG line
TRADE MARK REG.
ESTABLISHED SINCE 1933

24 PARTS

SCALE MODEL

DING HAO !

back to the Pacific to command his own Mustang unit during the invasion of Japan when the war came to a close.

An especially unusual tally of victory markings on a Mustang was under the cockpit rail of a P-51D named *Bad Angel*. Louis E. Curdes's airplane carried seven German swastikas, one roundel of the Royal Italian Air Force, a single Japanese rising sun flag, and, oddly, a single American flag.

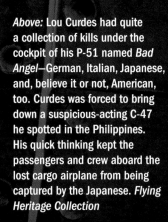

Most of his victories he achieved in the normal way—over the Mediterranean and then Formosa (today Taiwan). The American kill, however, requires more explanation. During a rescue mission off the island of Bataan in the Philippines, Curdes spotted a C-47 with American markings headed in to land at a Japanese-held airfield. Puzzled, he moved his Mustang in for a closer look. It soon became apparent that the cargo airplane was either under enemy control or it momentarily would be, if Curdes held his fire. He decided to shoot.

Still curious to find out who was flying this mystery airplane, Curdes aimed for the engines. The C-47 crash-landed in the waters offshore and twelve people, including two US Army nurses, piled into life rafts. When they were rescued, Curdes found out that the occupants of the C-47 were, in fact, all Americans.

They had become lost and were low on fuel. As Curdes came onto the scene, the pilots of the cargo airplane were unknowingly lining up to land on an enemy-held airstrip. The Mustang pilot's quick thinking had helped them all avoid becoming prisoners of the Japanese. Stranger still, Curdes had been out on a date with one of the army nurses on the doomed C-47 just the night before. He later told a reporter, "Jeepers, seven 109s and one Macchi [Italian fighter airplane] in North Africa, one Jap, and one Yank in the Pacific. And to top it, I have to go out and shoot down my girlfriend!"

Above: Lou Curdes had quite a collection of kills under the cockpit of his P-51 named *Bad Angel*—German, Italian, Japanese, and, believe it or not, American, too. Curdes was forced to bring down a suspicious-acting C-47 he spotted in the Philippines. His quick thinking kept the passengers and crew aboard the lost cargo airplane from being captured by the Japanese. *Flying Heritage Collection*

Left: A "Seastang?" The US Navy tested a tailhook-equipped P-51D on the carrier USS *Shangri-La* in November 1944 with a number of takeoffs and landings. The Mustang's efficient wing made it a bit worrisome at slow landing speeds required for a carrier. In addition, the US Navy preferred air-cooled engines for its carrier airplanes. With American forces tightening the noose on Japan every day, there would soon be no need for "Seahorse fighters." *Robert Elder/Nicholas A. Veronico*

Above: Colonel William Banks, commander of the 348th Fighter Group, flies *Sunshine VII* in the last weeks of World War II. The rainbow nose on the P-51K carried the color of each of the four squadrons within the group, and the large black stripes on the airplane helped in quick recognition from nearly any angle. *The Norm Taylor Collection/The Museum of Flight*

Opposite: NAA loved to show off its Mustang. When the D model went into service, advertisements like this proudly touted the P-51's characteristics. The tagline: "Unmatched in speed, ceiling, and combat radius, Mustangs fight from Burma to Berlin." *The Museum of Flight*

three fighters and the bomber on his first pass, the major turned to face his attackers and brought a fifth airplane down in a head-on pass and then dispatched two more as they attempted to run.

When it was over, Shomo and his recon Mustang, named *Snooks 5th*, had destroyed seven enemy airplanes; his wingman accounted for three more Japanese fighters, while the

remaining three retreated into a cloud bank. No USAAF pilot had ever achieved seven confirmed victories in a single day. For the action, Shomo became the second of three Mustang pilots to be awarded the Medal of Honor in combat. His citation reads, in part, "Maj. Shomo's extraordinary gallantry and intrepidity in attacking such a far superior force . . . is unparalleled in the Southwest Pacific area."

What would become the main event in the Pacific took place well north of the Philippines. Soon after US forces came ashore in the Marianas Islands in the summer of 1944, they quickly began creating huge airfields for long-range bombers. Basing B-29s in China had proven too difficult, and the raids from remote airfields in Asia were often unsuccessful. But now there was another option.

The islands of the Marianas (Saipan, Tinian, and Guam) would be the home base for hundreds of US Army bombers—all within striking distance of the home islands of Japan. In

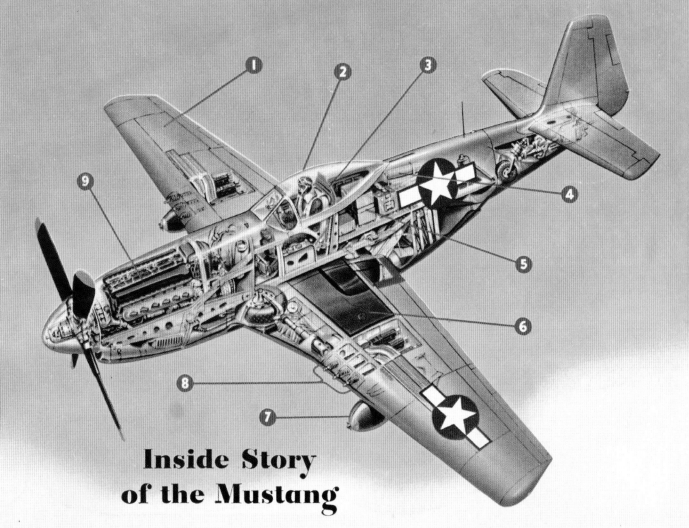

Inside Story of the Mustang

Here are nine reasons why the P-51 Mustang is the most efficient, most deadly, most feared American fighter-plane in enemy skies:

1. **REVOLUTIONARY DESIGN**—laminar-flow super-speed wing.

2. **NO BLIND SPOTS**—full vision cockpit enclosure.

3. **ARMOR PLATE**—this bullet-proof seat back protects Mustang pilots.

4. **FIGHTS EIGHT MILES UPSTAIRS**—these tanks provide oxygen for pilot.

5. **TWO-WAY RADIO**—provides close coordination during missions.

6. **SELF-SEALING GAS TANKS**—an important safety factor in combat.

7. **BOMB LOAD**—1000 pounds under each wing.

8. **DEADLY FIREPOWER**—six .50 cal. machine guns, three in each wing.

9. **SPEED—OVER 425 MPH**—1520 HP supercharged engine and automatic, variable pitch propeller.

North American P-51 Mustang Fighter

Unmatched in speed, ceiling and combat radius, Mustangs fight from Burma to Berlin

North American Aviation *Sets the Pace*

PLANES THAT MAKE HEADLINES...*P-51 Mustang fighter (A-36 fighter-bomber), B-25 and PBJ Mitchell bomber, AT-6 and S.N.J Texan combat trainer, and the B-24 Liberator bomber. North American Aviation, Inc. Member, Aircraft War Production Council, Inc.*

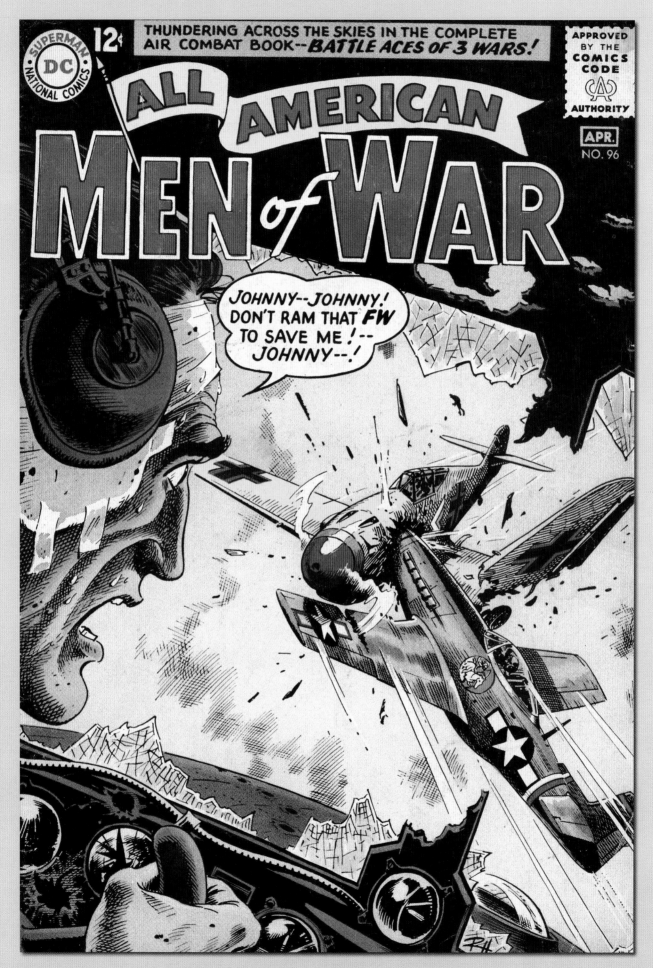

November of 1944, heavy bombers left the Marianas and struck Japan for the first time. Their target was an airplane plant on the outskirts of Tokyo.

In many ways, the initial B-29 raids looked a lot like those in Europe; large formations of bombers at high altitude, in daylight, made precision strikes on industrial targets in Japan. American crews encountered modest defensive action in the form of fighters and antiaircraft fire. The only thing missing to complete the picture of these "traditional-style" bombing missions was squadrons of escort fighters. As 1945 dawned, American planners began eyeing the small volcanic island

outpost of Iwo Jima in order to add Mustangs to their missions over Japan.

Iwo Jima was approximately 750 miles from Tokyo, just close enough to allow P-51s, fueled to the gills, to make the grueling eight-plus-hour roundtrip flight with the big bombers. In one of the bloodiest and most famous battles of World War II, US Marines took control of Iwo Jima in late February and March 1945. Soon after, USAAF units moved in with their P-51D Mustangs.

The first "very long range" (VLR) mission from Iwo Jima took place on April 7, 1945. Mustangs of the 15th and 21st

Above: How does a pilot go to the bathroom on an eight-plus-hour trip over the Pacific? It's not well known, but the Mustang came equipped with a funnel and tube. Disappointingly, the P-51's flight manual refrains from any amusing details on how to use it. It simply states, "The relief tube is stowed on a bracket on the floor of the cockpit at the left of your seat." *Flying Heritage Collection*

Opposite: Men of War's hero, Navajo ace Johnny Cloud, flew a P-51D that had a strange mix of heraldry from the Pacific, Europe, and Korea. And that Focke-Wulf on the cover is actually a Messerschmitt! Interestingly, art from the comic series was the inspiration for one of American pop artist Roy Lichtenstein's best-known works, *Whaam!*, which featured a Mustang blasting a jet fighter. *Author's Collection*

Above: The Mustang's fuel-selector valve allowed a pilot to pull from one of the airplane's three internal tanks or two drop tanks. Combat pilots learned about one flaw in the system. Periodically the selector switch would break off in a pilot's hand, leaving him with fuel, but no way to get to it. Some savvy pilots carried pliers in their pockets for just such an occasion. *Flying Heritage Collection*

Inset: The men of the Seventh Air Force were assigned to the Central Pacific during the last years of the fight against Japan. Mustang units flew from Iwo Jima to the Japanese Empire in some of the longest fighter missions of the war. *Author's Collection*

Above: Indeed. A popular home-front slogan meant to encourage conservation of fuel and rubber with the family automobile is transferred to the cowling of a Mustang with comedic results. Seeing crews unloading drop tanks for the long flight to Japan in April of 1945, I'd say, yes, at least this time, you're going. *National Archives*

Opposite: Mustangs, bound for Iwo Jima, pack the deck of the escort carrier USS *Kalinin Bay*. The airplanes of the 506th Fighter Group went to Hawaii and then Saipan. From there, USAAF pilots made the final flight to Iwo Jima on their own. Sailors and pilots worked together to get the maximum number of airplanes onto the flight deck of the small vessel. *National Archives*

Right: A formation of 15th Fighter Group Mustangs leaves Saipan on March 7, 1945. The airplanes are headed to their new home in the middle of the Pacific, the small island of Iwo Jima. From there, the P-51s could escort Boeing B-29 bombers as they hit targets in Japan. *National Archives*

MUSTANG P_51 D

MISS JACKIE

311

436/912

CETTE BOITE VOUS OFFRE LA POSSIBILITÉ DE RÉALISER AU CHOIX 2 VERSIONS DE CET APPAREIL.

Heller
Echelle 1/72ème

Above: In the 1960s, French model maker Heller released this version of the P-51D featuring Iwo Jima–based *Miss Jackie*, or N2-E, of the 364th Fighter Group in England. *Author's Collection*

Left: Navigational B-29s were assigned to shepherd Iwo Jima–based Mustangs to Japan. Here, *Joltin' Josie* of the 498th Bomb Group leads six flights of 15th Fighter Group P-51s to targets near Tokyo. *National Archives*

Opposite: Japan attempted to build new airplanes that could challenge high-flying B-29s and prowling Mustang fighters. The Nakajima Ki-44 "Tojo" and the Ki-84 "Frank" were capable airplanes, but lack of production capacity and abbreviated pilot training made the average Japanese fighter ineffective against American air forces by 1945. *Author's Collection*

Finishing Touch

An American Mustang pilot has latched himself onto the tail of a new Nip Navy plane—the Tojo. The frantic Jap has pulled every trick in the book. Finally, in desperation he racks his Tojo into a back-breaking 180 degree vertical turn. The Mustang pilot refusing to give up his advantage, follows. Halfway around the Mustang has out-turned the Tojo. At the three-quarter mark the Jap has turned into the gun sights of the Mustang. The American pilot applies the "finishing touch."

BONDS bought these planes ★ WASTE FATS helped arm them ★ WASTE PAPER helped ship them ★ GASOLINE flies them ★ WILL YOU help deliver the next squadron?

◀ "Hurricane Hall," famed wind tunnel at North American Aviation where engineers create man-made hurricanes to develop and test the stability and flight characteristics of the P-51 Mustang.

North American Aviation *Sets the Pace*

PLANES THAT MAKE HEADLINES... *the P-51 Mustang fighter (A-36 fighter-bomber), B-25 and PBJ Mitchell bomber, the AT-6 and SNJ Texan combat trainer. North American Aviation, Inc. Member, Aircraft War Production Council, Inc.*

Above: A 506th Fighter Group Mustang is pushed over pierced steel planking in the dispersal area on Iwo Jima. Note the double antenna behind the cockpit. The airplane's "Uncle Dog" system helped Mustangs navigate over endless miles of ocean and return home. When a pilot strayed to one side of the flightpath, he heard the Morse code letter D ("dog" or "dah dit dit"). If he strayed to the other side, he heard U ("uncle" or "dit dit dah"). *National Archives*

Right: A companion turns to shoot a photo of his wingman as they pass over Mount Suribachi. The costly battle to take Iwo Jima took more than a month and took the lives of more than 6,800 US Marines. Afterward, the island airbase became a hub of activity in the Central Pacific. *7th Fighter Command*

Dixie Boy served with the North Dakota and Illinois ANG in the years after World War II. The airplane, in a worn civilian paint scheme, sat outside for decades in San Jose before being fully restored in the early 2000s. *EAA/Jim Koepnick Photo*

Fighter Groups escorted bombers headed to Tokyo and Nagoya. And while P-51 pilots claimed 101 Japanese airplanes shot down, two Mustangs failed to return.

It soon became apparent that combat over the Japanese mainland was only a fraction of the overall picture of the Central Pacific air war. Flying a tiny Mustang over hundreds of miles of ocean was far more dangerous. Problems with fuel, navigation, fatigue, or weather were much more likely to bring down a Mustang than any hastily trained Japanese pilot in the final months of his defense of his homeland. These dangers were brought to the forefront in June 1945, when 150 Mustangs were led into a storm by a navigation bomber during an escort flight to Osaka, Japan. Thrown about in the clouds, planes collided with one another, and all but twenty-seven of the 150 P-51s that started the mission aborted. Back on Iwo Jima, twenty-six pilots and

their airplanes never returned—lost without so much as firing a shot.

In the last months of the war, the tactics of the American bombers changed, and the threat of enemy airplanes dwindled to nearly nil. As B-29s took to area bombing by night, the Mustang pilots were left to make their own sweeps of targets in Japan in daylight. Regardless of the mission type, the long trip to and from Japan remained the same: hauling two 110-gallon drop tanks, six high-velocity aircraft rockets (HVARs), and a full complement of ammunition, the Mustangs would take off for Japan—a trip farther than a flight from London to Berlin and back. After hours of mind-numbing boredom as the hot sun beat down, the P-51 pilots had a few minutes to raise hell over the Japan's home islands, shooting up airfields, exploding factory buildings, or hammering supply trains and barges with their guns and rockets. One Iwo Jima-based Mustang pilot

This Peace Talk Makes Sense

You don't have to translate the language of a Mustang's 50 calibre guns or the 75 millimeter cannon talk of a Mitchell bomber. The Japs already understand. So do the Nazis. So let's keep talking, You bet you can help! Think of it this way. The Bonds you buy help build these fast-talking planes. The waste fat you collect helps arm them. Waste paper helps ship them, and gasoline flies them. Wouldn't you like to say a few words of this kind of "peace talk," too?

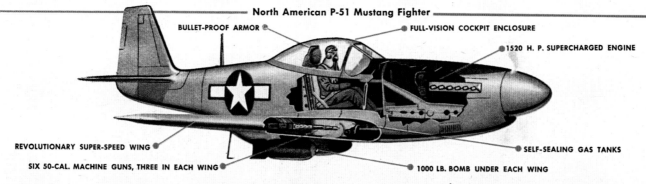

North American P-51 Mustang Fighter

BULLET-PROOF ARMOR •   • FULL-VISION COCKPIT ENCLOSURE

• 1520 H. P. SUPERCHARGED ENGINE

REVOLUTIONARY SUPER-SPEED WING •

• SELF-SEALING GAS TANKS

SIX 50-CAL. MACHINE GUNS, THREE IN EACH WING •   • 1000 LB. BOMB UNDER EACH WING

THE MUSTANG IS A FIGHTER FROM THE GROUND UP!   Speed: over 425 m.p.h.   Ceiling: 40,000 feet   Range: 2000 miles

North American Aviation *Sets the Pace*

PLANES THAT MAKE HEADLINES . . . *the B-25 Mitchell bomber, AT-6 Texan combat trainer, P-51 Mustang fighter (A-36 fighter-bomber), and the B-24 Liberator bomber. North American Aviation, Inc. Member, Aircraft War Production Council, Inc.*

Above: A 21st Fighter Group P-51D Mustang shot on Guam by Harold Gronenthal. The airplane to the left is an SB-17 rescue airplane. In the far background is a B-29 of the 504th Bomb Group. *7th Fighter Command*

Opposite: As the conflict in Europe escalated, casualties increased dramatically over the four months prior to the release of this September 1944 ad. Americans yearned for peace. Wearied by the continued conflict in the final year of the war, the public was reminded by manufacturers such as NAA to continue to fund efforts with bonds. The "Japs and Nazis" only understood force, says the ad. "You don't have to translate the language of a Mustang's .50-caliber guns." *Author's Collection*

encountered a Japanese warship in Osaka Bay and exploded its front magazine solely with .50-caliber gunfire.

When historians analyze the use of Mustangs from Iwo Jima, they are mixed in their assessment of the airplanes' usefulness. The long distances to Japan and difficult conditions, combined with the change in tactics for the bombers, leave many to question how critical the capture of Iwo Jima was and whether it should have been bypassed and left isolated. This alternate version of the final days in the Pacific might have meant a quicker invasion of areas nearer to Japan, more suitable for single-engine fighters. Nevertheless, areas surrounding the island of Okinawa fell to US forces in April and June of 1945, and Army flying units moved in almost immediately.

In order to protect bomber groups of the Pacific air forces (along with elements of the Eighth Air Force arriving from Europe), airfields on Okinawa, along with the small island of Ie Shima, became overrun with Mustangs and Thunderbolts. One of the first Mustang units was the 35th Fighter Group, formerly based in the Philippines.

The war ended before most Mustang units in the Okinawa area got the chance to get started. Some of the Mustangs were hoisted aboard ships and brought back to the United States. Most in the military had no idea that, in half a decade, some of the Mustangs would be moved back across the Pacific for the next US war.

6

SOLDIERING ON

AT THE END OF WORLD WAR II, the United States had thousands of combat-ready airplanes and millions of USAAF personnel. Outside America's aircraft factories, busy workers finished more airplanes by the hour. In this new, seemingly odd era of peace, a different kind of purge began: the US government slashed airplane contracts to nearly nothing. NAA went from ninety-one thousand workers to five thousand in just one year. Most of the bloodlines of the famous airplanes that helped win World War II were abruptly ended only days after Japan's surrender in August 1945. Moving forward, there would be no more AT-6 Texan trainers, no more B-25 Mitchell bombers, and, for the most part, no more Mustang fighters.

Many of the airplanes already purchased and accepted by the USAAF fared no better. In the Pacific, some perfectly good airplanes were pushed into ravines by Army bulldozers.

This F-51D, seen serving with the Minnesota Air National Guard in the 1950s, still flies today. The airplane was part of Minnesota and Montana ANG units before becoming a Cavalier conversion bound for Guatemala in 1962. Upon return, the airplane was restored as *Miss Marylyn II* and is today registered to a private owner in Texas.
Al Hamblin/Nicholas A. Veronico

Mr. Lucky, a P-51D of the 355th Fighter Group, is photographed in Gablingen, Germany, in July 1945. After World War II, several England-based units moved to German airfields. The colorful stripes on the tail of the fighter are the symbol of the US Army of Occupation. *Flying Heritage Collection*

In Europe, mighty bombers were dynamited in their parking spots for scrap. In a matter of weeks, transport ships were no longer needed to bring supplies to the battlefields across the Pacific but to bring troops and equipment home. In this new world, seamen on outbound vessels literally dropped brand-new airplanes into the sea in order to clear the way for homeward-bound troops. The USAAF purged its inventory of airplanes from sixty-three thousand to thirty-four thousand airplanes in the first twelve months of peace.

Yet there was some method to the liquidation. Military leaders worked hard to save some of the most valuable airplane types from destruction. The long-range Boeing B-29 Superfortress bombers had the potential to become valuable tools for keeping the Soviets in check. Douglas C-47 transports could be converted to passenger airplanes and used in the civilian market. And Mustangs, along with some P-47 Thunderbolts, were still considered to be some

of the most valuable and versatile piston-powered fighters of the era.

Jet airplanes were clearly the future of military aviation. But as with any kind of new technology, these new, high-tech airplanes were complex, expensive, and troublesome in the last years of the 1940s. During the transition from prop-driven airplanes to jets, proven commodities like the venerable Mustang would have to do.

National Guard units in the United States took many Mustang and Thunderbolt fighters after World War II. Generally, squadrons in the East and South flew the Republic P-47s, while those in the West and Midwest operated Mustangs. Just as the P-51s were often veterans of wartime, so too were the pilots who filled National Guard rosters, delighted to fly with their beloved Mustangs for a few more years.

In 1947, the US Air Force (USAF) was officially formed from the ranks of the USAAF. During this time of transition,

Rows of F-51s stretch into oblivion at the San Antonio Air Material Center at Kelly Air Force Base around 1949. From here, many Mustangs found homes with ANG units, while others were sold to foreign nations at bargain prices. Still others were brought back to life for regular USAF service during the Korean War. *USAF via The Norm Taylor Collection/The Museum of Flight*

the United States struggled to create an improved inventory of airplanes to tackle new types of missions; countering the Russians over very long distances with the use of air-dropped nuclear weapons, as well as preparing for the possible outbreak of another tactical war in Europe. The Mustang had enough range and versatility to be retained for both scenarios. But there were some changes. Months after the transition of the USAAF to the USAF, army Mustangs officially went from being designated P-51s ("P" for "pursuit") to F-51s ("F" for "fighter").

When North Korean forces pushed beyond the 38th parallel on June 25, 1950, some of the first American airplanes thrown into action were Japan-based two-seat F-82G Twin Mustangs of the 68th Fighter Squadron. On June 26, F-82 pilots guarding a convoy of evacuating civilians encountered North Korean fighter airplanes but chose not to engage them, wanting not to endanger the scores of refugees on the ground below. On June 27, however, the Twin Mustang pilots fired their first shots of the war. Lieutenant William G. Hudson and his radar operator, Lt. Carl Fraser, pounced on an attacking Yak fighter near Kimpo airfield. At close range, Hudson fired his six .50-caliber guns while Fraser hurriedly tried to photograph the history-making event with his malfunctioning thirty-five-millimeter camera. This engagement was the first aerial victory of the Korean War. Two other F-82 pilots shot down enemy airplanes during this combat as well.

The Twin Mustangs were used only briefly. While they were suited to the task at hand, there were only 168 of them in the USAF inventory at the beginning of the Korean War, and they could only be supported for around sixty days. By contrast, there were more than 1,500 F-51 Mustangs available—764 in Air National Guard (ANG) units and 794 more in storage. The first group of 145 Mustangs, recalled from ANG units, was already on its way, tightly packed on the flight deck of the carrier USS *Boxer*.

Capability and availability had much to do with the USAF decision to send F-51s to Korea, but another important variable was cost. Cynical USAF pilots were quick to point out that the price tag for an average Mustang from the factory

This photo shows a trio of F-51Ds assigned to the ANG's 144th Fighter Group. Each squadron within the group flew in a separate state: the 192nd Fighter Squadron out of Las Vegas, Nevada; the 191st Fighter Squadron from Salt Lake City, Utah; and the 194th Fighter Squadron flying from Alameda, California. During Korea, the airplane in the foreground served with the South African Air Force and the Republic of Korea Air Force. *William T. Larkins/Nicholas A. Veronico*

Above: This ANG F-51D was photographed in 1951. The airplane served with the California, Illinois, and New Hampshire ANGs before being shipped to Nicaragua in 1963. The airplane was restored and owned by enthusiasts in the United Kingdom and the United States until 1995. The Mustang, named *Sunny VIII*, was destroyed in a crash at an airshow in Malone, New York, in July 1995. *Al Hamblin/Nicholas A. Veronico*

Inset: With jets clearly the wave of the future, Mustangs filled the gap in ANG units during the transition years of the 1950s. *Author's Collection*

during World War II was $50,000. The airplanes were ready, reasonably well suited for primitive runways, numerous, and, importantly, paid for. By contrast, a Lockheed F-80 cost the US government twice as much, and an NAA F-86 rolled out from the factory floor at nearly four times the price of a vintage Mustang.

For the second time in less than a decade, Mustangs were going to war.

In combat in Europe during World War II, the P-51 was most often used as an air superiority weapon that commonly escorted American bombers, engaging any Luftwaffe threats. At the beginning of the Korean War, F-51s were first considered dual-role fighters. While they could effectively fight any of North Korea's World War II–era Soviet-built airplanes that challenged them, the F-51s were primarily used as bomb haulers.

Above: In March 1950, this F-51 ended up lodged in the wall of a coffee shop at Nellis Air Force Base in Nevada. Most likely, the airplane never flew again. And why would it? In those months before the start of the Korean War, there were more Mustangs in the world than anyone knew what to do with. *National Archives*

Right: It seemed odd to call the P-51 the F-51. The creation of the USAF changed "pursuit airplanes" to "fighters." The Mustang, along with a handful of other late-1940s combat airplanes, had to make the transition. *The Museum of Flight*

AIR FORCE

F-51

MUSTANG

NORTH AMERICAN AVIATION, INC.

Mustangs came to the front in two- and four-ship elements and made contact with a forward air controller or troops on the ground. Often, North Korean forces would fade away into the landscape and attempt to wait it out when a squadron of airplanes armed with bombs appeared overhead. It was in this exact situation that the F-51 had another advantage over jet airplanes: Jet-powered F-80s could handle the job of ground attack, but they could only stay in the area for about fifteen minutes before running low on fuel. By contrast, a flight of Mustangs might be able to loiter for five times as long, allowing the battle below to develop and lucrative targets to reveal themselves. At this point, the Mustangs went to work, lobbing five-hundred-pound bombs or napalm at T-34 tanks, tearing into columns of trucks with five-inch rockets, and strafing troops with their .50-caliber guns.

Strafing and launching HVARs required aiming the weapons through the Mustang's K-14 gunsight. Some pilots liked to give a short burst of fire from their guns as they started their dive to the target; though they were out of range, they hoped that the noise and sight of the flame-spitting Mustang would help induce enemy gunners to keep their heads down instead of firing at the incoming airplanes. Pilots also learned to use their rudder and stick to slip or slide in unnatural ways as they dived for targets. A slewing Mustang was much harder to hit than one flying "right down the chute."

The tactics for bombing were somewhat more involved. Lines painted on the wings of the Mustang, radiating out from the cockpit, helped a pilot gauge when to start his bomb run. Flying offset from the target, when the aim point passed under the stripe for the airplane's corresponding altitude, the pilot would roll over and pull into a sixty- to seventy-degree dive heading directly at the aim point. As the target disappeared under the nose of the fighter, the pilot would check his needle and ball instrument to make sure he was flying briefly "centered" and then toggle his bombs, usually at around two thousand feet. He would then race away from the area, often zigzagging over nearby terrain as cover until a mile or more from the aim sight. Finally, trading airspeed for altitude, the

continued on page 173

Texas ANG Mustangs, flying from Kelly Air Force Base near San Antonio. After World War II, many F-51s in ANG units operated with their tail wheels permanently locked down to minimize maintenance. Texas F-51Ds flew painted as a squadron of Republic of Korea Air Force Mustangs in the 1957 Rock Hudson movie *Battle Hymn*. Santa Maria Museum of Flight

"MODERN MUSTANGS"

After the end of World War II, most Mustang production came to an end. Some 8,102 NAA P-51Ds and 1,500 P-51Ks had been built before the long assembly lines closed down in Texas and California in late summer 1945. Programs to produce radically improved versions of the Mustang were also undertaken during the war years. Lighter, faster, and stronger Mustangs, designated P-51Hs, were built to serve in the Pacific in the last year of the war. Approximately 2,000 had been ordered by the army, but only 370 were rolled out from the factory in Inglewood before the Japanese surrender. A total of 555 were produced before the assembly line closed down for good.

Another version of the Mustang developed during the wartime era was the P-82. Long flights over the Pacific took their toll on a lone pilot in the sweltering cockpit of his fighter. Designed to combat this, the P-82 "double Mustang" looked like two P-51 fuselages grafted together, and it gave a pilot some relief on incredibly tedious eight-plus-hour missions. Based on F and H versions of the P-51, the P-82 was, in reality, an entirely new airframe designed from scratch. The airplane made its first flight in June of 1945, but the end of the war put the P-82 project into limbo as the initial order for 480 of the airplanes was cancelled.

However, Cold War needs brought the Twin Mustang back into production the following year. The threat of Russian long-range bombers coming over the North Pole, as well as the

T.O. No. 1F-51D-1
(Formerly AN 01-60JE-1)

RESTRICTED

FLIGHT HANDBOOK

PILOT TRAINING MANUAL FOR THE F-51D

Mustang

RESTRICTED

The Pilot Training Manual for the F-51D is a trove of information on the airplane. This version, printed in 1954, includes loads of illustrations, graphs, and even cartoons on the subject of the famous and, by that time, nearly decade-old combat airplane. *Flying Heritage Collection*

The quirky, kooky Aurora P-51 Mustang model kit was an F-51H made out the hardest green styrene known to man. Sold in the mid- to late 1950s, the kit was quite popular for its time. Perhaps you too recall opening the box and finding the airplane's insignia, buzz numbers, and a thousand rivets heavily embossed into the plastic pieces! *Author's Collection*

A flight of H-model Mustangs assigned to the 57th Fighter Group cruise over the rugged landscape of Alaska. The airplanes were serving as part of the Alaskan Air Command and were positioned to intercept Russian bombers. While they had the range, they lacked radar to track Soviet threats and were soon replaced. This shot was taken in April 1948. *National Archives*

need to escort American nuclear-armed attackers deep into Russian territory, made the P-82 a valuable tool for the Strategic Air Command. Other versions emerged from the factory built as radar-equipped night fighters to replace outgoing Northrop P-61 Black Widows.

That said, the entire P-82/F-82 program was a stopgap measure. Just 272 of the airplanes were built before new jets could take their place. But Twin Mustangs, in the right place at the right time, flew the first missions of the Korean War and claimed the first victories over North Korean foes in air-to-air combat.

While the P-82 was envisioned as a two-man airplane from the beginning, NAA artist Reynold Brown was tasked with rendering this two-engine, one-pilot double Mustang. Brown went on to be an accomplished movie poster artist, creating imagery for *How the West Was Won*, *Creature from the Black Lagoon*, and *Attack of the 50-Foot Woman*. *Santa Maria Museum of Flight*

How much gear can they hang on one Twin Mustang? A lot. This image shows the XP-82 loaded to the gills with two five-hundred-pound bombs, ten five-inch rockets, and fourteen .50-caliber machine guns. Other test arrangements on the airplane included rockets, guns, and three one-thousand-pound bombs. *Santa Maria Museum of Flight*

Above: With a load of rockets and napalm, a South African Air Force F-51D gets ready for an early-morning takeoff. The tips of Mustang propellers were painted yellow to keep a ground crewman from getting too close to a spinning prop. The echo in the middle of the propeller disc is made by the airplane's Hamilton Standard decals. *National Archives*

Following pages: At an overhaul shop in Korea, F-51 Mustangs undergo heavy maintenance in 1951. The airplanes in the center, with teeth, are unmistakably 18th Fighter-Bomber Wing airplanes (12th Fighter-Bomber Squadron), one of which is having its radiator changed out due to ground-fire damage. The airplane farthest from the camera is a Royal Australian Air Force 77th Squadron fighter. *National Archives*

continued from page 168
F-51 pilot would steeply climb back up to the relative safety of the skies.

During the bombing process, the F-51s were dangerously exposed. Operating only a few hundred feet from enemy troops presented lots of opportunities to catch a bullet or shard of shrapnel in the Mustang's vulnerable coolant system. A vast majority of the 341 F-51s lost in Korea due to enemy action were shot down by gunfire from the ground. In order to protect themselves, Mustang pilots developed a system whereby one pilot would attack while another rode "shotgun" from two thousand feet or more, known as a yo-yo maneuver.

The pilot flying top cover could look for muzzle blasts directed at the lower fighter and dive in to suppress the most dangerous weaponry spotted below.

Key bridges and tunnels were important targets to stem the flow of North Korean troops. These fixed locations often had some of the heaviest antiaircraft weaponry standing in wait for the Mustang fighter-bombers. Making matters worse, these tunnels and bridges were in many cases set into deep valleys, which allowed gunners to predict the most likely approach points and even shoot downward at American airplanes. These "flak traps" often shot down American airplanes, killing pilots, which seemed even more senseless

when the North Koreans opened up the route soon thereafter and troops could easily move again.

On November 1, 1950, a group of Soviet-built MiG-15 jet fighters swooped in on fifteen Mustangs engaged in a ground-attack mission. Mustang pilot 1st Lt. Aaron R. Abercrombie became the first victim of the new-to-combat MiGs when his F-51D was shot from the skies. Mustang pilots claimed that three MiGs were damaged in the scuffle, but none of the more modern, faster, jet-powered Soviet fighters were destroyed.

Eight days later, during another confrontation, two F-51 pilots of the 36th Fighter-Bomber Squadron claimed damage to MiGs while Harris Boyce of the 35th Fighter-Bomber Squadron was credited with a probable kill.

Above: An armorer installs a fuse into the nose of a five-hundred-pound bomb hung from the pylon of a 35th Fighter-Interceptor Wing F-51D. Note the wire at the noses of the rockets. These arming wires were set to activate the warheads of the HVARs when they flew from the airplanes. *National Archives*

Opposite: "Tough, fast, hard-hitting, and elusive," the Mustang returned to Asia as an attack airplane during the Korean War. Though this ad appeared six years before Korea, nearly nothing had changed. Though now, F-51 pilots had to be on the lookout for prowling MiG-15 fighters as they went about their work hitting enemy strongholds below. *Author's Collection*

Right: This ANG F-51 gives a good view of the aids painted on the wings to assist in bombing runs. This particular airplane sold as surplus in 1957 for $790! The airplane flew with many owners until 1992, when it was destroyed in a crash as the civilian owner rolled the airplane too close to the ground. *Santa Maria Museum of Flight*

Following pages: Loads of dented and dirty seventy-five-gallon drop tanks, modified to carry napalm, lie in the foreground as F-51s carrying five-hundred-pound bombs head off on another mission over Korea. The tanks, left over from World War II, were used to deliver the fuel and gel mixture. On a busy day, USAF units dropped more than forty-five thousand gallons of napalm in Korea. *National Archives*

Mustangs on the Warpath

The forward element is peeling off. The other half of the squadron will fly formation during the attack, providing top cover. That's how P-51 Mustangs take to the warpath over Burma. And what a hunting ground it has been. Hunting with everything from bazookas to 500 pound depth charges and 1,000 pound demolition bombs, Mustang pilots have forced the Jap in Burma to move furtively at night and to hide in the jungle during the day.

Like its famous namesake the P-51 Mustang is tough, hard-hitting and elusive.

North American Aviation *Sets the Pace*

PLANES THAT MAKE HEADLINES... *the P-51 Mustang fighter (A-36 fighter-bomber), B-25 and PBJ Mitchell bomber, AT-6 and SNJ Texan combat trainer. North American Aviation, Inc. Member, Aircraft War Production Council, Inc.*

With the appearance of the MiG-15, any illusions of Mustangs valiantly dogfighting in the skies over Korea in anything other than cases of self-defense quickly faded. Protected from above by more capable F-80s and F-86s, the Mustangs went about their work, "moving mud" near Red Army units below, their pilots always keeping a wary lookout for speedy, jet-powered MiGs.

While they could never win in an out-and-out duel, American pilots soon developed tactics to counter state-of-the-art jets should their Mustangs be "bounced" while in the midst of their ground-attack work. If a Mustang followed the series of maneuvers precisely, he could survive the encounter. By practicing against friendly F-80s, F-51 pilots learned to turn sharply into an attacking jet as it came into range to use its guns. This put the MiG nose to nose with the slower fighter, nullifying the MiG's speed advantage, and allowed the Mustang pilot a brief head-to-head shot at the attacking fighter. After the MiG zoomed by, the Mustang

Above: These days it seems every P-51D left in the world flies with a scheme from World War II Europe. Not so for the Heritage Flight Museum's *Val-Halla*. The airplane is decidedly postwar, complete with high-visibility panels, buzz number, and post-1946 national insignia. *Historic Flight Museum*

Below: Using a modified trolley, a five-hundred-pound bomb is positioned near *Dottie*. The veteran F-51D flew in combat with the 35th Fighter-Interceptor Wing, 18th Fighter-Bomber Group, and then the Republic of Korea Air Force. The airplane was lost in combat in March 1954. *Stan Piet Collection*

An F-51D sloshes through a puddle on the way to the runway in Korea. Robert "Pancho" Pasqualicchio's 18th Fighter-Bomber Group Mustang, named *Ol' NaDSOB*, stood for "napalm-dropping SOB" and carried a small drawing of him and his airplane going to work. Pasqualicchio flew more than 350 combat missions in Korea. The airplane, serial 45-11742, was the very last P-51D produced by NAA. It was lost in Korea in October 1951. *National Archives*

Following pages: F-51s of the 18th Fighter-Bomber Wing are parked in the arming pits before a mission as pallets of five-inch HVAR rockets stand nearby. The airplane on the left was lost in combat on New Years Day 1952. *National Archives*

Right: Crews load seventy-five-gallon tanks filled with napalm. An igniter went in the place of the tank's filler cap. Safety wires, affixed to the airplane, pulled from the igniter when the tank dropped away from the airplane, arming the weapon. *Stan Piet Collection*

Opposite: Though created during World War II, this ad still held true during Korea. The Mustang, as fighter-bomber, again became an effective and useful weapon in Asia more than a decade past its prime. *Author's Collection*

pilot turned his airplane over and headed for the deck in a steep corkscrewing dive. Should the jet finish its sweeping 180-degree turn and come back before the Mustang made it to the ground, the F-51 pilot again turned to meet his assailant face-to-face with guns blazing.

Once down amid the mountainous terrain, it was difficult for the MiG to match the Mustang's slow speed and turning ability to get in position for a dead-to-rights tail-on shot. Jet pilots preferred to stay high, making slashing attempts at the more maneuverable prop-driven fighter below. On each pass, the slower-moving Mustang would turn, raise, and fire at the MiG as it thundered past. The Mustang pilot usually didn't have to wait long before the MiG was out of fuel and had to head for home. When it departed, the Mustang could retreat as well. This act of self-preservation didn't earn a Mustang pilot any medals, but it did allow him to fight again another day.

One F-51 pilot, however, did earn the nation's highest military honor during combat actions in Korea. Major Louis J. Sebille was the first of four USAF pilots to receive the Medal of Honor for service in Korea. During an attack near Taegu on August 5, 1950, Sebille's Mustang was damaged by antiaircraft fire while on a bomb run, and his airplane began to trail

smoke. He radioed his wingman and reported that he was hit and wounded badly. His companions urged him to set out for a nearby emergency airfield, but Sebille turned back toward the enemy. "I'll never make it," he reportedly told his comrades. He radioed, "I'm going back and get [*sic*] that bastard."

Rockets zooming from the wings of his Mustang, Sebille flew his mortally wounded fighter and its remaining five-hundred-pound bomb into a convoy of North Korean troops and armored vehicles. His Medal of Honor citation states, in part, that "Major Sebille . . . dived on the target to his death. The superior leadership, daring, and selfless devotion to duty which he displayed in the execution of an extremely dangerous mission were an inspiration to both his subordinates and superiors and reflect the highest credit upon himself, the U.S. Air Force, and the armed forces of the United Nations." Sebille became the first member of the USAF to receive the Medal of Honor and the third Mustang pilot to receive the award.

The grim business of slowing North Koreans' advance went on for months. USAF pilots knew they could not fly an antique forever, at least not in combat. Though F-51 pilots and their trusty airplanes from a bygone era held their own and made life miserable for the enemy, the Korean War was taking its toll on both men and machines. Working only a few

Winged Javelin

Starting in a screaming dive at 8,000 feet this P-51 Mustang pilot is hurling his winged javelin at a Jap artillery position. Right now he is travelling so fast that anti-aircraft guns cannot even follow him. He is in an 80 degree dive. His pull-out will be at "rhubarb height." This is one of the most accurate forms of bombing. The strain on both plane and pilot is terrific, but the P-51 Mustang can take it like American pilots can dish it out.

BONDS bought these planes.
WASTE FATS helped arm them.
WASTE PAPER helped ship them.
GASOLINE flies them.
WILL YOU help deliver the next squadron?

North American Aviation *Sets the Pace*

PLANES THAT MAKE HEADLINES...*the P-51 Mustang fighter (A-36 fighter-bomber), B-25 and PBJ Mitchell bomber, the AT-6 and SNJ Texan combat trainer. North American Aviation, Inc. Member, Aircraft War Production Council, Inc.*

Right: Lieutenant Frank Buzze of the 18th Fighter-Bomber Wing knows he's had another close one. A Mustang pilot who flew in the Pacific during World War II, and then in Korea, he was hit on an attack mission in August 1950. One bullet, fired from the ground, punched a hole in his seat and lodged in the carbon-dioxide cylinder of his seat-pack life raft. *National Archives*

Inset: Mustangs flew and fought with the Fifth Air Force twice—first during World War II and later in Korea. Quite a number of the F-51 pilots who wore the Fifth Air Force's distinctive comet insignia on their shoulders in Korea had flown fighters in Europe, the Pacific, or the CBI years before. *Author's Collection*

hundred feet over the frontlines day after day, the venerable Mustangs collected a lot of holes, or worse.

Maintenance personnel, toiling away in the dirt, mud, and snow at the most primitive and desolate airfields, began to joke that the "Spam can" F-51s were more punctures, patches, and bailing wire than actual original airplane. As the war progressed, the majority of Mustangs were phased out of combat in favor of jet airplanes. The 8th Fighter-Bomber Group was first to make the switch, trading its Mustangs for F-80 Shooting Stars in December 1950; in 1951, two more combat units, the 35th Fighter-Interceptor Group and the 49th Fighter-Bomber Group, also made the leap to jets. By the fall of 1951, the only USAF ground-attack unit still operating F-51s was the 18th Fighter-Bomber Wing. It flew its weary Mustangs until early 1953, when they were finally relieved of combat operations. Many of the pilots of the 18th were in the odd position of being expert pilots of piston-engine fighters in an air force that had moved on to jet airplanes years before. Some moved to F-86 training while others were reassigned to other Fifth Air Force units, including some that went on flying Mustangs in support of the Republic of Korea Air Force.

Korean pilots and some USAF reconnaissance pilots continued to fly their F-51s until the end of the fighting. In all, F-51 Mustangs in Korea dropped 12,909 tons of bombs and fired 183,034 rockets at the enemy. They were the critical key, particularly in those early days of fighting in 1950, to slowing and then stopping the North Korean advance to Pusan.

Stateside, F-51s continued to serve with Air National Guard units until 1957. Immediately after the war, the ANG had sixty-five fighter-bomber and fighter-interceptor squadrons still flying F-51D and F-51H airplanes. Four recon squadrons operated RF-51Ds as well. By way of comparison, just two squadrons were equipped with F-47s at the end of Korea, and the entire ANG had taken delivery of just six jet airplanes.

By 1955, only eight ANG squadrons still flew Mustangs as the transition to jets was fully underway. In January of 1957, the last F-51D in USAF tactical service was transferred from the 167th Fighter-Interceptor Squadron of the West Virginia ANG to what was then called the United States Air Force Museum in Dayton, Ohio. The age of the Mustang's regular service in the US military was done.

This last F-51, serial 44-74936, was met over Ohio by an NAA F-100 Super Sabre and escorted to Patterson Field for an impromptu air show. The Mustang flew again the following month over Marietta, Ohio, for the premiere of the movie *Battle Hymn* before being permanently retired.

Curators chose to display the airplane as it would have looked during World War II, painting it to represent a P-51D named *Shimmy IV*, flown by Col. C. L. Sluder, commander of the 325th Fighter Group in Italy in 1944. The name of Sluder's airplane was a combination of the names of his daughter, Sharon, and his wife, Zimmy. Today, *Shimmy IV* can still be seen on display in the World War II gallery of the museum.

Left: A pair of California ANG pilots prepare their F-51H Mustangs for flight in 1953. The H-model Mustangs were incorporated into the unit when the demand for F-51Ds ramped up due to actions in Korea. In 1954, the F-51H Mustangs were replaced with another NAA product, the F-86A Sabre jet fighter. *Al Hamblin/Nicholas A. Veronico*

Opposite top: On January 27, 1957, Maj. James Miller parks the final F-51 used in regular USAF service at Wright-Patterson Air Force Base. The airplane, with its modest-size nose art, *Wham Bam!*, is today on display at the National Museum of the US Air Force. *National Archives*

Opposite bottom: The last Mustang in regular USAF service was retired to the US Air Force Museum in 1957. Today, the name has changed to the National Museum of the US Air Force, but the airplane is still there, displayed in a place of honor in the World War II Gallery. *National Museum of the US Air Force*

7

STAYING POWER

AFTER 1957, MANY P-51 MUSTANGS became museum pieces, though not all. Some of the most significant, history-making airplanes reside today in institutions in the United States and abroad. The oldest surviving Mustang is proudly displayed at the AirVenture Museum of the Experimental Aircraft Association (EAA) in Oshkosh, Wisconsin.

This airplane, XP-51 serial 41-038, was the last of four prototypes built by NAA in 1940 and the first P-51 acquired by the US Army Air Corps. It was tested in Dayton, Ohio, before being transferred to the National Advisory Committee for Aeronautics in December of 1941. After World War II, it was held by the Smithsonian National Air and Space Museum (NASM) in Washington, DC, until the 1970s, when it was turned over to the EAA Aviation Foundation in a trade and restored to flyable condition in Colorado. The restoration

The Planes of Fame P-51A (43-6251) was recovered from a technical school in Glendale, California, a year after World War II ended. This image shows the airplane after its 1981 restoration for flying condition. Since, the rare airplane has changed identities, becoming *Mrs. Virginia* of the 1st Air Command Group. *Nicholas A. Veronico*

Above: It's hard to miss this Mustang when it flies by. *Sparky*, a P-51D (44-72777) sports a Jelly Belly–sponsored scheme during races in the mid-2000s. The airplane served in Italy during World War II and went to Indonesia in 1967 as a Cavalier II. Back in the United States, the airplane appeared in an HBO movie and was flown for years in airshows. According to the airplane's website, this Mustang got its name when "Steve (Seghetti) landed it after forgetting to deploy the landing gear. Sparks shot up from the bottom of the airplane and the name *Sparky* was born." *Mark Stevens*

Left: The fourth Mustang built now resides at the EAA AirVenture Museum in Oshkosh, Wisconsin. It was supplied to the USAAC for evaluation in the buildup to World War II. The rare airplane is the oldest Mustang in existence. *Zachary Baughman, EAA AirVenture Museum*

Paul Mantz's P-51C, NX1204, as it appeared in 1949. The airplane was returned to its "blood red" scheme for the year's Bendix race. The airplane finished second with an average speed of more than 450 miles per hour. The airplane is owned today by Kermit Weeks. *The Peter M. Bowers Collection/ The Museum of Flight*

process was extremely difficult because 41-038 was built so early in the production run and many of its parts and components for the rare fighter were still built by hand when it emerged from the factory floor. Restorers found that there were no accurate drawings of the type, and airplane technicians discovered that NAA had used many AT-6 parts to complete the airplane as quickly as they could. The restored airplane flew for the first time in 1976 and wowed audiences at air shows in Oshkosh until 1982, when it was retired.

Just three of the five hundred A-36 Apache airplanes produced survive today. *Margie H*, today located at the National Museum of the United States Air Force, has a post–World War II history in air racing. The A-36A was acquired by pilot Kendall Everson and Essex Wire Corporation after the US Army released the weary former attack airplane. Everson flew the Apache, then named *City of Lynchburg II*, in the five-lap, 105-mile Kendall Oil Company Trophy Race in Cleveland in 1947.

The field was all ex-military built by NAA—five P-51s, Everson's A-36, and another A-36A flown by Woody Edmundson. Edmundson was in the lead until his Allison began to fail in the fourth lap; his airplane was wickedly smashed when he attempted a belly landing and hit a tree. Everson's A-36 moved into second place while a P-51D piloted by Steve Beville rumbled over the finish line first. Beville's newer Mustang clocked 384.602 miles per hour in the race, while Everson's Allison-powered attack airplane came in at 377.926 miles per hour.

The A-36 (often dubbed a P-51A by race organizers) raced again in 1949 with Jack Hannon at the controls. After pulling out in the seventh lap of the Tinnerman Trophy Race, the airplane took last place among the finishers in the R Division Thompson Trophy Race (300.396 miles per hour). The rare airplane was acquired by the United States Air Force Museum and restored back to its wartime appearance by the Minnesota Air National Guard soon after.

Top: After a record-setting dash across the United States, the press mobs a Mustang pilot who flew from Los Angeles to New York in six hours, thirty-one minutes, and thirty seconds. The sprint included a stop of six minutes and twenty-five seconds in Kansas City for fuel. The P-51D averaged 390 miles per hour. *National Archives*

Above: Here's a blast from the past. The *Phantom Mustang* started many a love affair with the P-51/F-51 among generations of kids. In addition, the iconic kit taught many a young man to hate . . . how to hate model glue. One cannot count the number of Christmases that were ruined when someone got a little out of control with the Testors plastic cement. Every ten or fifteen years, it seems, this model is reissued just in time to flummox a new group of model builders. *Emil Minerich*

Right: How do you tell if all the cylinders are firing? Get your hand up there. A crewman checks the Merlin of P-51B racer *Thunderbird* in 1949. The airplane was co-owned by Joe DeBona and actor and pilot Jimmy Stewart. That year the airplane won first place in the Bendix race, at a speed of 470 miles per hour. *Santa Maria Museum of Flight*

This well-traveled P-51C (44-10947) has been known by *Stormy Petrel*, *The Houstonian*, *Blaze of Noon*, and of course, *Excalibur III*. Today, Paul Mantz's Mustang hangs in a place of honor at the National Air and Space Museum's Steven F. Udvar-Hazy Center in Virginia. The museum first took possession of the airplane in 1953. *Author's Collection*

Currently, 3 of the 310 P-51A airplanes built for the US Army are still in flyable condition. Amazingly, two of them are parked a few hundred feet apart from each other at a pair of aviation museums both located in Chino, California. *Mrs. Virginia*, a former instructional airframe at Glendale's Cal-Aero Technical Institute, resides at the Planes of Fame Air Museum. Nearby, Yanks Air Museum displays another Allison-powered Mustang that stayed stateside during the war. After a brief stint as an air racer in 1948, the latter airplane was restored in the 1970s. Today, it is seen in F-6B configuration, equipped with F24 cameras behind the pilot's seat.

Only seven P-51B/C-type Mustangs remain out of the 3,737 built during wartime. Perhaps most famous among these are a pair of P-51Cs once owned by Hollywood stunt flyer and former army pilot Paul Mantz, who purchased about five hundred surplus military airplanes in Oklahoma in 1946 for

$55,000. The squadrons of airplanes, including eight Mustang fighters, made Mantz briefly the holder of the world's sixth largest air force.

While there were some ninety P-40 Warhawks and thirty-one P-47 Thunderbolts, only a handful of Mustangs were deemed saleable by the Reconstruction Finance Corporation. They were "razorback" C models built in Dallas—considered too old to be of any use for the military.

Many locals scoffed at the foolishness of the man from California and his unmanageable fleet of "worthless" airplanes. First Mantz sold the fuel found inside the derelict airplanes, making a profit. He then stripped the engines, Plexiglas, and oxygen regulators and sold those, too. Finally, he had most of the airplanes cut up for scrap, making money on that endeavor as well.

Mantz kept only twelve of the airplanes. Two of them were "blood red" P-51C Mustangs he used to dominate the cross-country air racing circuit in the years immediately after the war. Mustang NX1202 flew to victory in the two-thousand-plus-mile Bendix Trophy Race with Mantz at the controls in 1946; the flight from Los Angeles to Cleveland took Mantz four hours and forty-six minutes. NX1204, flown by Thomas Mayson, came in third, arriving in five hours and one minute. A year later, Mantz and NX1202 came in with another win, beating his previous time by several minutes. His average speed was over 460 miles per hour. Mayson finished sixth in NX1204. That same year, Mantz used his Mustang to set coast-to-coast speed records going in both directions. In 1948, he took first prize in the Bendix yet again, this time piloting NX1204. Linton Carney, flying NX1202, came in second.

In 1949, Mantz's duo of racers was finally beaten by Joe DeBona, flying, of course, another Mustang. NX1204 and NX1202 came in second and third, piloted by Stan Reaver and

Herman "Fish" Salmon, respectively. Both thoroughbreds continued to set flying records after they left Mantz's hands.

In 1951, Capt. Charles F. Blair used NX1202 (named *Excalibur III*) to set speed records from New York to London (seven hours and forty-eight minutes), Fairbanks to New York (nine hours and thirty minutes), and over the North Pole from Bardufoss, Norway, to Fairbanks, Alaska (ten hours and twenty-seven minutes).

Mustang NX1204 was involved in a more bizarre speed dash in 1953 when NBC hired race pilot Stan Reaver to rush film footage of Queen Elizabeth II's coronation oath to the people of the United States. CBS recruited Joe DeBona and his Mustang to do the same. With the first- and second-place finishers of the 1948 Bendix ready to sprint one thousand miles from Labrador, where the film was being delivered by an RAF jet bomber, to TV studios in Boston, it was going to

One could argue that a vintage fighter airplane with a 1,500-horsepower engine is a bit much for a civilian to handle without the proper training. This P-51D (44-63507) ran into grief near Brownwood, Texas, in 1968. It was the second of three times this airplane would be involved in accidents during its civilian career. On each occasion, the rare airplane was brought back from the dead by warbird restorers. *The Norm Taylor Collection/The Museum of Flight*

Val-Halla, P-51D (45-11525), was once owned by USAF pilot and Apollo 8 astronaut Bill Anders. The airplane wears the scheme of the 57th Fighter-Interceptor Squadron, based in Iceland. Anders donated the airplane to the Heritage Flight Museum in 1996. The airplane's name is an amalgamation of Bill's wife's name, Valerie, and the Viking word for heaven. Anders's USAF call sign was Viking. *Lyle Jansma*

be a rematch of 1948's Bendix race. Once again, DeBona's Mustang (and CBS) won the flying contest, but NBC won the media race by making a last-minute deal to share the Canadian Broadcasting Corporation's feed while DeBona's P-51 still zoomed toward Boston.

Both iconic P-51s still exist today. NX1204 is owned by vintage airplane collector Kermit Weeks of Florida; the still-airworthy airplane now wears the colors of Tuskegee Airman Lee Archer Jr. NX1202 and hangs in a place of honor at the NASM's Steven F. Udvar-Hazy Center in northern Virginia.

Mantz's and Blair's record-breaking P-51C isn't the only Mustang held by the NASM. When this museum needed an archetypical American warbird for its World War II Aviation Gallery, it chose, of course, an NAA P-51D. The D-model Mustang was the winner of the warbird game. Nearly 3 percent of the 8,200 D models made in California and Texas

still exist today, and the P-51D is viewed by many warbird collectors as the '57 Chevy of the air—classic, iconic, and ridiculously popular.

Many celebrities own or have owned Mustangs throughout the years. Actor Tom Cruise flies *Kiss Me Kate*, a former K model restored as a two-seat TP-51D. Former NASA astronauts and USAF pilots Frank Borman and Bill Anders have restored, piloted, and possessed Mustangs, as has Richard Bach, author of *Jonathan Livingston Seagull*. Even former New England Patriot tight end Russ Francis was able to squeeze his six-foot-six, 242-pound frame into the tight cockpit of a Mustang he purchased in the 1980s.

Perhaps strangest of all, David Gilmour, guitarist and covocalist of the English progressive rock band Pink Floyd, owned and flew a former Texas ANG P-51D Mustang. He told the press he'd always been fascinated with the airplane,

CAVALIER

With the close of the Mustang's USAF service career, squadrons of the ex-fighters flooded the civilian market. One entrepreneur took advantage of the relatively inexpensive surplus airplanes to fill a need for civilians.

Florida publisher and Mustang fanatic David Lindsay Jr. hatched the idea of converting Mustangs into executive airplanes. The modified airplane could fly far and fast, getting a big shot (and his pilot) from state to state in minutes in the days before the Learjet was around to fill that role. Lindsay established Trans Florida Aviation Inc. to make the conversions in 1957.

Trans Florida's facility in Sarasota tore the Mustangs down completely, discarding military radios and weaponry. Workers then installed a plush interior, a second seat (in place of the fuselage radio equipment and fuel tank), new avionics, and an easily accessible luggage bay in each airplane. Originally called the Trans Florida Executive Mustang, the conversion was soon renamed the Trans Florida Aviation Cavalier Mustang. Over the years, many models were offered—the Cavalier 750, 1200, 1500, 2000, and 2500. Each designation indicated the approximate range of the airplane. On the exterior, the new, brightly painted airplanes often sported a tall, modified vertical tail, and the longest-range versions carried easily recognizable 110-gallon wingtip fuel tanks.

After many man-hours of work, Trans Florida could turn a worn-out F-51, purchased for a little as $950, into a sleek machine with a price tag that ranged from $18,000 to $32,000,

This Cavalier Mustang II, formally designated an F-51D-T.Mk2, ran into trouble near Robins Air Force Base in Georgia in June of 1967. The pilot reported magneto trouble before skidding to a muddy stop in an open field. The airplane was quickly rebuilt and furnished to the Bolivian Air Force in October 1967. *The Norm Taylor Collection/The Museum of Flight*

Seems like somebody's out looking for trouble. Cavalier Mustangs simply look wicked. This pair of Cavalier Mustang IIs is headed to El Salvador, circa 1968. They are photographed here over Sarasota, Florida, before making the trip south. FAS-404, nearest the camera, was returned to the United States and flown by a Texas flight museum until it was destroyed in a crash in 2013. FAS-405 still flies in Sweden. *Edward Lindsay/Nicholas A. Veronico*

depending on options. The problem was, very few people were buying. Only about twenty of the airplanes were sold to the pre–jet set crowd—the real money came from governments, not businessmen. In 1963, Trans Florida got the contract to inspect and repair thirty-one F-51s for the Dominican Republic. In 1967, after changing its name to Cavalier Aircraft Corporation, the company remanufactured a batch of Cavalier F-51D Mustangs for the US Department of Defense. Using a mix of surplus, new old stock, and newly produced parts, nine new airplanes went to Bolivia, while two more were retained by the US Army.

The next version was the Cavalier Mustang II, with updated avionics, strengthened structure, improved powerplant, and additional hard points for weaponry. The United States furnished some of these airplanes to El Salvador for close air support and counterinsurgency operations, while others went to Indonesia in 1967 as part of Operation Peace Pony.

A third iteration of the Cavalier Mustang incorporated a Rolls-Royce Dart 510 turboprop engine. The Turbo Mustang III touted better performance and lower maintenance costs, but Lindsay failed to garner interest from the USAF or foreign nations. In 1970, he sold the modified Mustang and the rights to produce it to Piper Aircraft.

Piper's version of the Mustang III flew with a Lycoming YT-55 engine and was named the PA-48 Enforcer. The USAF bought two for evaluation, but the project never gained any traction, and more airplanes were never produced. One of the surviving Piper-built Enforcers can be seen on display at the National Museum of the United States Air Force in Dayton, Ohio.

Lindsay's efforts did have one lasting effect on the Mustang community. Trans Florida saved many airplanes from the scrapyard, and those Mustangs, often reconverted to vintage-appearing airplanes, still fly today.

Lower left: The US Army obtained an F-51D (44-72990) to serve as a speedy chase airplane during the testing of the AH-56 Cheyenne attack helicopter in the late 1960s. The airplane's original serial number was changed to 0-72990—many joked that the 0 stood for "obsolete." The program was so successful, however, that the army added two Cavalier Mustangs to its fleet as well. The 72990 was the last Mustang used in all US military service, retiring in 1978. *Santa Maria Museum of Flight*

Lower right: Splashy covers are the bread and butter of the comic business, along with a healthy dose of advertising! It is always interesting to see how artists blend models and styles of Mustangs to come up with their own mixed creations. *Author's Collection*

Above: There's not much that *Ridge Runner III* (44-72483) hasn't done. The P-51D served with the 354th Fighter Group in Europe during World War II and in Nicaragua after. Back in the United States, the airplane raced regularly at Reno and suffered a forced landing in 1982. Today the airplane is based in Minnesota. *Nicholas A. Veronico*

Inset: Though other events have tried to best Reno, it remains the world's premier air racing event. And, even if you don't have enough cash to start a racing team, there are still plenty of ways to spend a little money picking up pins, programs, and yes, patches. *Author's Collection*

having built miniatures of the famous US fighter as a child growing up in Cambridge, England, right after the war. Fittingly, the collector who purchased Gilmour's airplane from him in 2003 named it *Comfortably Numb*—after the famous song Gilmour cowrote with Roger Waters.

Sadly, many of the airplanes saved from the scrapper's torch to fly today were those with the lowest amount of flight time at the end of the war. While wartime vets of combat over Europe and the Pacific were recycled wholesale, those that had just a few hours of flight time were saved. The NASM's P-51D never saw combat; it had only 211 hours of operational time before it was retired to become a museum piece. The airplane today depicts a veteran airplane of the 353rd Fighter Group named *Willit Run?*, that has long since been lost to history.

A few combat-veteran P-51Ds did survive destruction, often when they were supplied to another country at the end of the fighting. Ron Fagan of Granite Falls, Minnesota,

The P-51C named *Beguine* was heavily modified. Builders did away with the Mustang's distinctive belly scoop and instead cooled the airplane with radiators built into the wingtips. Observers described the airplane as dark, dark green, with an almost bluish tint to it. Bill Odem was killed when the airplane crashed during the 1949 Thompson Trophy Race. *Jim Pyle via A. Kevin Grantham Collection and Nicholas A. Veronico*

and the Flying Heritage Collection of Everett, Washington, both possess D-model Mustangs that served in the Eighth Air Force during World War II. Amazingly, both of these combat veterans shot down German Me 262 jet fighters during combat missions over Europe, and both were saved from oblivion when they were sold to the Swedish Air Force after the war. So were Mustangs named *Sierra Sue II* and *Ridge Runner III*, airplanes that served with the Ninth Air Force before also being sold to Sweden.

A handful of postwar P-51H and P-51K models still exist today, as do a number of former Cavalier and Piper Mustangs (see sidebar). A few of these airplanes are displayed in museums in their "natural" state, but so strong is the desire to own what appears to be a vintage P-51D that many collectors have "devolved" some more modern airplanes back to the way the Mustang would have looked during World War II.

Though the numbers are always changing, at any one time there are about 170 Mustang survivors in flying condition, around 60 more nonflying airframes on display in museums, and perhaps 60 more machines in storage, under repair, or in

Opposite, top: Talk about famous Mustangs . . . *Ole Yeller* has flown countless air-show performances and was used as the pace and safety airplane at Reno for twenty years. At the start of each Unlimited race, test pilot and airshow performer Bob Hoover would announce those famous words, "Gentlemen, you have a race," as he put his yellow Mustang into a steep climb to avoid the heavy traffic coming down "the chute." *Mark Stevens*

Opposite, bottom: They match! LeRoy Penhall's Lockheed T-33 and former Royal Canadian Air Force P-51D sport the same sharp color scheme in a photo probably taken in the early 1970s in Chino, California. Penall bought and sold a number of jet trainers in his day. The Mustang—that was an airplane he owned for fun. *Santa Maria Museum of Flight*

Below: At the height of the Vietnam War, there was a short-lived trend of offering distinctive, nonmilitary paint schemes and gaudy parts in airplane model kits. This racing Mustang with the hypothetical name of *Cleveland Miss* fits the bill. The airplane came with chrome-coated parts, clear "modular display stand," and enough funky decals to make your airplane model look just like your big brother's van. *Author's Collection*

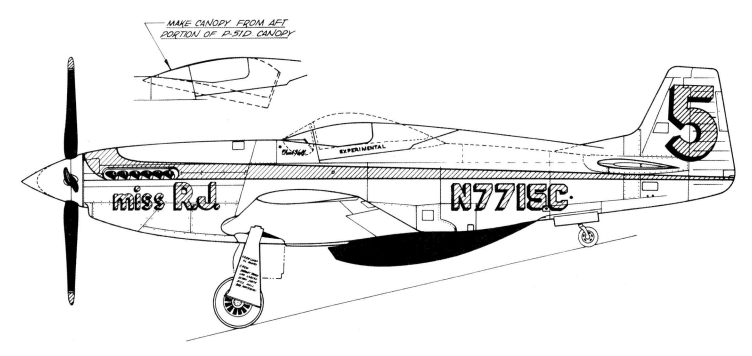

MAKE CANOPY FROM AFT
PORTION OF P-51D CANOPY

This drawing of air racer *Miss R.J.* shows some of the adjustments made to a stock Mustang to squeeze out more speed—aerodynamic spinner, clipped wings, and built-up aft fuselage. Designers found an inexpensive way to incorporate a low-profile canopy by turning the airplane's original canopy around and chopping it down. *The Museum of Flight*

Following pages: *Miss R.J.*, photographed around 1969. The airplane went on to be the *Roto-Finish* and *Red Baron*. In its final form, the airplane set the world piston-driven speed record in 1979 and was destroyed less than a month later in a crash. *Santa Maria Museum of Flight*

the midst of restoration. Of the more than 15,000 Mustangs built, about 1.8 percent of them have survived long enough to see the seventy-fifth anniversary of the prototype.

Interestingly, the Mustang named *Ridge Runner III* was not only a combat vet but flown as an air racer, too. Vintage Mustangs have been the dominant force in racing since they were let out into the civilian market in 1946. In the years immediately following World War II, the Mustang was the cross-country air racing king, winning the Bendix Trophy every year from 1946 to 1949. In those same years, Mustangs battled it out around the pylons in the famous Thompson Trophy closed-course race as well. Though often nudged from the top spot by other former military types, pilot Anson Johnson managed to claim top prize in the Thompson race in 1948 piloting a P-51D at 396 miles per hour.

The following year, a tragedy involving a Mustang would put the sport of civilian air racing on hold for a decade and a half. The 1949 Thompson race pitted six Mustangs against three Goodyear F2G Super Corsairs and a Bell P-63 Kingcobra. A dark green P-51C dubbed *Beguine*, flown by New Jersey native Bill Odem, was race number seven that day. During the race, Odem lost control of his airplane and dived into a house in the Cleveland suburbs, killing a young mother, a toddler, and the pilot himself in a fiery crash. It was the end of the National Air Races in the city of Cleveland and the end of civilian air racing until 1964.

A decade and a half later, air racing returned near Reno, Nevada. From a dusty two-thousand-foot airstrip at Sky Ranch, airplanes once again took to the air to roar around the pylons. In this modern era of Unlimited Class racing, the Mustang, once again, is king.

In a never-ending quest to turn faster laps, the former military airplanes have been highly modified to shave seconds off their lap times. Almost without exception, military radios, guns, and armor have been cast aside to lighten the load. New blends of fuel, high-performance propellers, and nitrous oxide injection systems soon followed. More radical physical modifications have also been introduced by speed-obsessed pilots: chopped wings, tiny streamlined canopies, and entirely new powerplants make some P-51s look like only shadows of their former wartime appearance.

Of the seventy-four Unlimited races that have taken place since 1964 at Reno and beyond, Mustangs have claimed first prize forty-two times. Their fiercest competition

Chuck Lyford readies for an early morning flight in the *Bardahl Special* P-51D (44-84390) in August 1965. That year, Lyford and his Mustang won two Golds; at Lancaster, California, and Boulder City, Nevada. He came in second at Reno in 1965. *Jim Larsen*

Omni/Lacy... right on!

Above: P-51D (44-15651) *Galloping Ghost* was a fixture of the air-racing circuit for decades. This image clearly shows the degree to which racers "chopped" the wingtips of original Mustangs to make them faster. During a race at Reno in 2011, one of *Ghost*'s elevator trim tabs tore free, causing longtime owner and pilot Jimmy Leeward to lose control of the airplane and crash. *Jim Larsen*

Opposite: Clay Lacy's P-51D Mustang (44-74423) got its distinctive color in a peculiar way. Someone ordered 1,500 gallons of the paint by accident. Soon, everything at California Airmotive was getting coats of the distinctive "orchid" purple. Then owner Allen Paulson told Lacy, "People remember purple," and so their Mustang became purple, too. As *Miss Van Nuys*, the Mustang won Reno in 1970 with Lacy in the cockpit. The purse for the race was $7,200. *The Museum of Flight*

comes from newer, highly modified Grumman F8F Bearcat racers, which have won twenty-three competitions during the same timespan.

In that first race in 1964, three Bearcats battled four Mustangs for top honors. A P-51D named the *Bardahl Special* piloted by Bob Love qualified with the fastest time, at 395.46 miles per hour. But it was Myra Slovak, piloting an F8F sponsored by Smirnoff Vodka, who won the competition, collecting more race points on the weekend in a complicated heat system that was quickly abandoned. That inaugural race set up , speedy Mustang that lasts to this day.

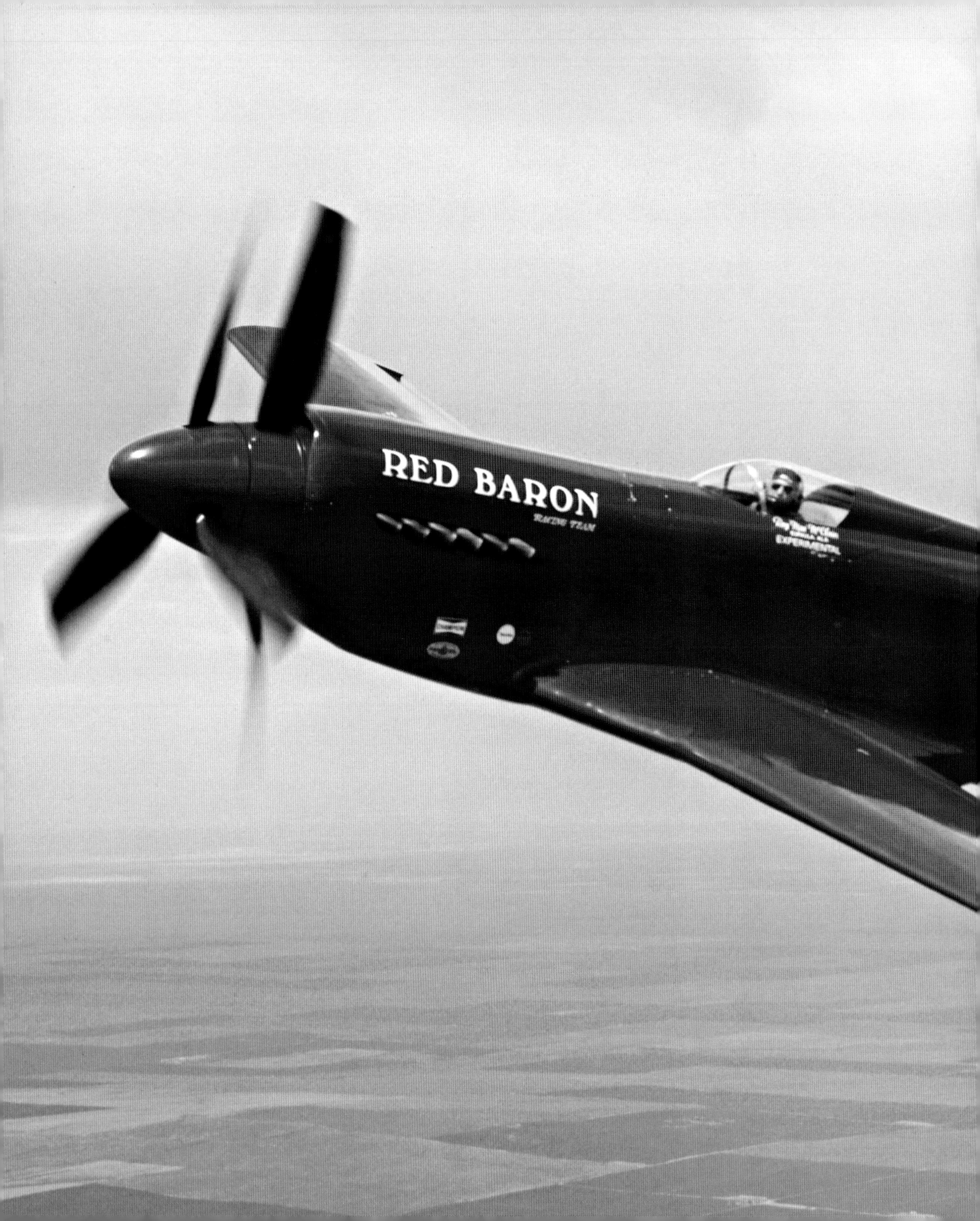
RED BARON
RACING TEAM
EXPERIMENTAL

Above: When is a Mustang not a Mustang anymore? When it never was. *Tsunami* was a purpose-built racer powered by a Rolls-Royce Merlin V-12. While smaller than a Mustang, the racing airplane still has a little of that familiar look to it. *Tsunami* was fast, but the unique machine was lost in a fatal accident in 1991. *Santa Maria Museum of Flight*

Left: In its time, *Red Baron* was one of the fastest piston-powered airplanes in the world. This shot was taken around 1976, a few years before the airplane's record-breaking speed run. Coupled with its highly modified airframe, the airplane's Rolls-Royce Griffon engine and contra-rotating propellers generated more than three thousand horsepower. *Jim Larsen*

While a heavily modified F8F named *Rare Bear* holds the record for the most Unlimited Gold Race wins in the modern era (sixteen), a trio of Mustang race airplanes—*Red Baron*, *Strega*, and *Dago Red*—hold the next three spots on the list and account for twenty-seven Gold Race wins between them. *Dago Red* holds the record for the fastest six-lap race ever flown at over 507 miles per hour.

The first of these three Mustang super-racers was *Red Baron*, a P-51D built in Dallas and sold as surplus in 1958. The airplane began its race career in the mid-1960s, flying with many of the modifications that would become standard on nearly all competitive Mustang racers, including clipped wings, a reduced-profile canopy, and a modified prop spinner. Though it was fast and competitive, winning Gold at Reno in 1972 as the *Roto Finish Special*, the airplane's most significant changes were yet to come.

In the mid-1970s, a new owner replaced the D model's Merlin engine with a three-thousand-horsepower Rolls-Royce Griffon V-12 taken from an Avro Shackleton bomber and added

This great shot from a wing-mounted camera shows *Voodoo* passing a pylon on the eight-mile Unlimited course at Reno around 2000. The former US Army and Royal Canadian Air Force P-51D (44-73415) has had quite a career as a racer. As of the time of this writing, *Voodoo* has been the Reno Unlimited Gold Champion for two years (2013 and 2014). *Jim Larsen*

a pair of contra-rotating propellers and a bigger vertical fin. Now named *Red Baron*, the Mustang racer was a monster in the making. Indeed, this airplane took over the sport, winning in 1976 (Mojave) and 1977 (Reno). With pilot Steve Hinton at the controls, *Red Baron* claimed the top prize at Reno (1978), Miami (1979), and Mojave (1978 and 1979). Over Tonopah, Nevada, twenty-seven-year-old Hinton set the piston-driven airplane three-kilometer world speed record with *Red Baron* at 499.047 miles per hour in August of 1979.

Red Baron met its end in the Nevada desert a month later, on Sunday, September 16, at the Reno Air Races. An in-flight magneto failure was soon followed by the destruction of the airplane's supercharger and oil pump. Hinton crash-landed the P-51 short of the runway, and *Red Baron* tumbled among the rocks and burst into flame. Hinton was badly hurt in the crash but survived; *Red Baron* was a total loss. The pioneering Mustang racer had claimed wins in seven Gold Races and held the world speed record before being lost.

Another P-51D was similarly stripped, chopped, and fared by racers in the early 1980s. Though builders took many aerodynamic cues from *Red Baron*, they elected to keep a Merlin engine in *Dago Red*. However, that Merlin V-12 was anything but stock. Instead of the 1,500-horsepower engine used in World War II–era P-51s, *Dago Red* flew with a high-powered model taken from a postwar Canadian transport airplane. Loaded down with additions and improvements, high-octane fuels, and a huge dose of hot-rodding know-how, *Dago Red*'s engine could make 3,600 horsepower or more.

Bill "Tiger" Destefani is fond of naming his airplanes with Italian monikers. His first Mustang was *Mangia Pane*—"bread eater." Most P-51 owners will agree that Mustangs do, in fact, consume lots of your "bread." *Strega* means "The Witch." Though consistently fast and competitive, the airplane has recently been put up for sale or sponsorship. *Jim Larsen*

The airplane was a success, winning six Gold Races over three decades with three different pilots. The year of the last win, 2003, pilot Skip Holm flew *Dago Red* on a Friday Gold race at Reno at a jaw-dropping six-lap speed of 507.105 miles per hour. There has never been a faster time for a modified World War II Unlimited racer.

The third racing Mustang, *Strega*, has won more Gold races than *Dago Red* and *Red Baron* combined. Cut from the same cloth as the others, the former Royal Australian Air Force airplane began its historic three-plus-decade win streak in 1985. All told, *Strega* has rumbled across the finish line first fourteen times.

This handful of Mustangs are still out there earning a living some seventy-five years after the first P-51 was built. Many people have tried to find or create something that can go faster, but, as they say, "nothing beats a Mustang."

FAMOUS AIRCRAFT OFTEN BECOME SYMBOLS of the nations that built them. North American P-51 holds this place in the United States.

The story of this iconic airplane is so resonant to Americans because it is a narrative that embodies the stories and traits we value. Its history began with the opportunity to help an ally in need. It continued with a heavy dose of can-do spirit, coupled with creative genius, which together made the fighter plane a reality. With the unstoppable might of American industry producing this amazing machine for nearly every theater of World War II and brave pilots risking everything in daring duels in the skies, the future of the world hanging in the balance, how could one not be enthralled? And then there's the idea of power. An important part of the Mustang's allure was its ability to exert power

At some point, the P-51 Mustang's image evolved into a symbolic version of itself, mixed in with the imagery and themes of the United States and freedom. To alter Göring's famous Mustang quote: "When they started making Mustang commemorative plates and patches, I knew the war was lost." *Author's Collection*

Left: The NAA P-51 Mustang and the Ford Motor Company's Mustang sports car are part of the identity of the United States. Many people don't know that the automobile got its name from the famous fighter of World War II. In 2013, a one-of-a-kind 1967 Shelby GT500 "Super Snake" sold at an auction for $1.3 million. It was the most expensive Ford Mustang purchase of all time. These days, that's about the price of a marginal P-51 Mustang restoration project. *Historic Flight Museum*

Sun club . . . the Nautilus . . . the Roney Plaza Hotel . . . the sights go by fast as pilots race down Miami Beach in a Mustang at over 390 miles per hour. The numbers seen on the side of post–World War II airplanes were there to prevent unauthorized speedy, low passes over public areas. They were called "buzz numbers." This photo was taken in September 1946. *National Archives*

over great distances. Like it or not, that narrative is similar to that of the modern United States, even well after the Mustang fighter has become an antique.

The name "Mustang," as well, was chosen by the British because it reminded them of the United States: the wild horses of the Southwest were clever, strong, wild, and free. Years later, the same name was used when Ford Motor Company built another famous Mustang. Though Ford often focuses on western or patriotic iconography in its advertising, it was the company's executive stylist and lead designer, John Najjar, who originally suggested the name for the 1962 concept sports car. In an interview years later, Najjar recalled, "I'd been reading about the Mustang fighter plane. I was a nut for fighter planes—the P-51. I started to look at the name Mustang and

wrote it down a couple of times, looked in the dictionary, and I said, 'Geez, that's got to be it!'"

Interestingly, Ford could not use the name Mustang in Germany. Not because it brought up too many wartime memories or was too closely associated with the United States, but because the German company Krupp, a wartime builder of tanks and guns, had already produced a truck with the same name some ten years before.

Today, seventy-five years or more after the iconic plane first rolled off the assembly line and into combat, the image of the Mustang has become nearly a caricature of its former self. One can find images of this famed fighter on commemorative dishes, license-plate holders, lighters, and stamps, not to mention a deluge of models and toys. The plane has become

Loaded with gas, P-51D *My Girl* gets the signal to launch on the island of Iwo Jima. Several hundred miles from Japan, Mustangs of the 506th Fighter Group joined two other Mustang units on VLR missions in the last year of the war. *National Archives*

This "hero shot" shows a pilot and his Mustang, circa 1944. The photo was taken at Hickam Field, Hawaii, before the man and his airplane were deployed to combat, flying from Iwo Jima. *7th Fighter Command*

an iconographic staple of World War II movies, whether as a memorable scene-stealer in Steven Spielberg's 1987 *Empire of the Sun*, a savior in the 1998 *Saving Private Ryan*, or the star of George Lucas's 2012 *Red Tails*.

Today, real Mustangs are so rare and expensive that several companies have sprung up to supply replicas to amateur pilots who have several thousand dollars to spend in lieu of a few million. Commonly, these kit planes are smaller and relatively more powerful than the warplane they are meant to depict. Perhaps the most elaborate is the Cameron P-51G, whose carbon-fiber-epoxy airframe is the same size as the

original Mustang and flies with a 1,450-horsepower turbop-rop engine.

Purists, of course, argue that nothing comes close to the real thing. Vintage P-51s are the cornerstone of any museum collection of World War II aircraft. And these days, it seems, if you want to win Reno, you'd better have a Mustang. As of this writing, no plane other than a modified P-51 has won gold at that race since 2007.

Why is the P-51 Mustang so beloved? No one sums it up better than USAAF ace Capt. Richard Turner from Bartlesville, Oklahoma: "It's the best damn ship I have ever flown."

Above: Lieutenant Clark Clemmons of the 78th Fighter Group poses near the nose of his P-51D *Frances Dell* in April 1945. He flew nineteen combat missions during the war, including an encounter with a Messerschmitt Me 163 rocket fighter. After the war Clemmons continued to fly, becoming a pilot for United Airlines. *National Archives*

Left: What do you do when Messerschmitts are entirely too hard to get? Use something a bit closer to home. In the 1948 film *Fighter Squadron*, the good guys flew P-47 Thunderbolts, and Mustangs stood in for German Bf 109s. The repainted airplanes came from the 195th Fighter Squadron of the California ANG; their parent unit was sometimes called the "Hollywood Squadron" because of its frequent appearances on film. *Bruce Orriss*

INDEX

ACKNOWLEDGMENTS

No book is created by one person alone. I would like to thank the following individuals and institutions for their contributions to this volume: Amy Heidrick, John Little, Meredith Lowe Prather, Dan Hagedorn, and P. J. Müller at the Museum of Flight; P. Janine Kennedy; Calvin Graff; Erik Gilg, Madeleine Vasaly, and James Kegley at Zenith Press; the staff at the National Archives and Records Administration; Steven Hinton; Pete Law; Emil Minerich; Tim Nelson; Mike Lombardi of the Boeing Company Archives; and Adrian Hunt and the staff of the Flying Heritage Collection.

Special thanks to the people who donated so many of their wonderful images to this project: Jim Larsen; Heath Moffatt; Kate Simmons; Greg Anders; Lyle Jansma; Nick Veronico; Brett Stolle of the National Museum of the US Air Force; Marvin Baily of the Santa Maria Museum of Flight; Susan Lurvey, Jim Busha, Jim Koepnick, and Zack Baughman from EAA; Robert Dorr; Robert Elder; Al Hamblin; William Larkins; Pete Bowers; Norm Taylor; Edward Lindsay; Mark Stevens; Bruce Orriss; Michael O'Leary; Stan Piet; John Sessions; Liz Matzelle; and LaVone Kay. Without them, this book would have never been created.

This Mustang, P-51D (44-73420), was made at the end of World War II and served in the ANG. The airplane has changed hands through more than a dozen private owners over the years. Today, the airplane flies bare, as it would have looked when it left the factory. *Mark Stevens*